## Language

Stage directions
Verse, prose and rhyme
Figurative language                                54
Dominant recurring images                          55
Language and character                             57

## Themes                                          60

Kingship                                           60
Manhood                                            61
Good and evil                                      62
Appearance and reality                             63
Scotland - the health of the nation               65
Ambition and the supernatural                      66
Other themes                                       67

## Performance                                     68

The play in production                             68
- The director                                     68
- The actors                                       69
- Stage setting                                    71
- Costume                                          74
- Lighting and sound design                        75
- The play in performance                          75
- Film versions of the play                        76
- Filmed theatre productions                       78
- *Macbeth* on the Jacobean stage                  78

## Skills and Practice                             80

Skills for the assessment                          80
Sample questions                                   83
Sample answers                                     85

## Glossary                                        94

# Introduction

## What are Oxford Literature Companions?

Oxford Literature Companions is a series designed to provide you with comprehensive support for popular set texts. You can use the Companion alongside your play, using relevant sections during your studies or using the book as a whole for revision.

Each Companion includes detailed guidance and practical activities on:

- **Plot and Structure**
- **Context**
- **Characters**
- **Language**
- **Themes**
- **Performance**
- **Skills and Practice**

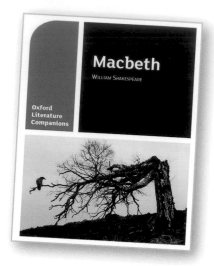

## How does this book help with exam preparation?

As well as providing guidance on key areas of the play, throughout this book you will also find 'Upgrade' features. These are tips to help with your exam preparation and performance.

In addition, in the extensive **Skills and Practice** chapter, the **Skills for the assessment** section provides detailed guidance on areas such as how to prepare for the exam, understanding the question, planning your response and hints for what to do (or not do) in the exam.

In the **Skills and Practice** chapter there is also a bank of **Sample questions** and **Sample answers**. The **Sample answers** are marked and include annotations and a summative comment.

## How does this book help with terminology?

Throughout the book, key terms are highlighted in the text and explained on the same page. There is also a detailed **Glossary** at the end of the book that explains, in the context of the play, all the relevant literary terms highlighted in this book.

## Which edition of the play has this book used?

Quotations have been taken from the Oxford University Press edition of *Macbeth*. (ISBN 978-0-19-832400-3)

# How does this book work?

Each book in the Oxford Literature Companions series follows the same approach and includes the following features:

- **Key quotations** from the play
- **Key terms** explained on the page and linked to a complete glossary at the end of the book
- **Activity boxes** to help improve your understanding of the text
- **Upgrade** tips to help prepare you for your assessment

To help illustrate the features in this book, here are two annotated pages taken from this Oxford Literature Companion:

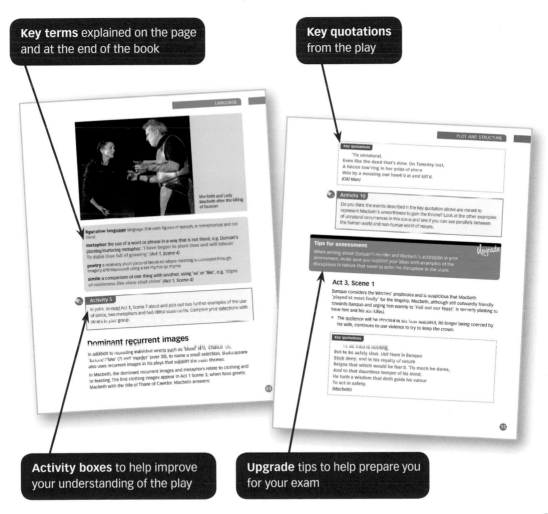

**Key terms** explained on the page and at the end of the book

**Key quotations** from the play

**Activity boxes** to help improve your understanding of the play

**Upgrade** tips to help prepare you for your exam

## Plot

### Act 1, Scene 1

Shakespeare plunges the audience into action near a battlefield, where Macbeth and Banquo lead the Scottish king's forces to victory against the invading Norwegians. A clap of thunder and lightning reveals the first characters of the play, the three Witches, who plan to **'meet with Macbeth'** once the battle is over.

- The Witches speak in **rhyme** and riddle: **'When the battle's lost, and won'**, chanting the **paradoxical** lines, **'Fair is foul, and foul is fair'**, before they disappear.
- The Witches' strange physical appearance and their use of riddles introduce the important theme of **equivocation**.
- The fact that Macbeth is known to these supernatural creatures is **ominous**.

**equivocation** the use of misleading, contradictory or ambiguous language intended to deceive others. The word is used a number of times in the play, especially in relation to the way the Witches deceive Macbeth into thinking he is invincible

**ominous** a warning sign

**paradoxical** contradictory or inconsistent ideas that are spoken as facts

**rhyme** a similar sound in the ending of words, e.g. trouble/bubble

The Witches have been presented in very different ways in stage and film versions of the play

**Activity 1**

The Witches have been presented in strikingly different ways in stage and film versions of the play: very old or very young, sometimes as men and sometimes as women. Research past productions on the Internet and discuss the dramatic effects of these different interpretations.

## Act 1, Scene 2

At his camp, King Duncan receives news of the bravery of Macbeth and Banquo against the invaders and how Macbeth has slain the rebel Macdonald. Duncan praises Macbeth as a **'valiant cousin, worthy gentleman'**. Ross and Angus bring decisive news of victory, reporting upon Macbeth's persistent courage and the defeat of the traitorous Thane of Cawdor. Duncan condemns the traitor to death and dispatches Ross to confer the title of **Thane** of Cawdor upon Macbeth.

- Duncan's praise of Macbeth's violent deeds provides an example of **proleptic irony** as Duncan himself will be killed violently by Macbeth, while Macbeth's own decapitated head is paraded at the end of the play.
- Duncan's final line, **'What he hath lost, noble Macbeth hath won'**, echoes the Witches' intentions to meet Macbeth, **'When the battle's lost, and won'** (*Act 1, Scene 1)* and emphasizes the **ambiguous** nature of conflict, where 'success' or 'failure' depends on the perspective of the individual.

**ambiguous** something that can be interpreted in different ways

**proleptic irony** irony that occurs when a character says something that turns out to be more significant than it appears at the time

**thane** a title given in medieval times to the Scottish equivalent of an English baron. The title, along with land, was granted to noblemen by the king in return for military service in wartime and advice during peace

**Activity 2**

The audience has yet to meet Macbeth in person. Discuss why you think Shakespeare has made him a subject of discussion in each of the first two scenes. Make a list of the things, good or bad, that we have learned about him so far.

# Act 1, Scene 3

On the heath, the First Witch is casting a spell upon the sailor-husband of a woman who has insulted her. Between them, the Witches have the 'ingredients' to create a storm at sea, making the captain's ship **'tempest-toss'd'** and rob him of sleep. At the sound of a drum beat, the witches prepare a charm for Macbeth.

As Macbeth and Banquo enter, the Witches greet Macbeth, first calling him Thane of Glamis, then Thane of Cawdor and then **'king hereafter'**. When Banquo asks them to prophesy his future, they predict that Banquo will father kings, **'though thou be none'**. They then vanish.

Almost immediately, Angus and Ross arrive to bestow the title of Thane of Cawdor upon Macbeth. In **soliloquy**, Macbeth considers the nature of the Witches' prophecy.

- The Witches are shown as vengeful and powerful, enjoying tormenting humans. This does not bode well for Macbeth.
- Macbeth's opening comment, **'So foul and fair a day I have not seen'**, eerily echoes the chant of the witches in Scene 1.
- Macbeth's reaction to the fulfilment of one of the Witches' prophecies is to believe instantly that he can obtain the crown, while Banquo cautions his friend about the dangers of meddling with **'the instruments of darkness'**, showing both his concern for Macbeth and for his own honour.

---

**Key quotations**

　　　But 'tis strange,
And oftentimes, to win us to our harm,
The instruments of darkness tell us truths;
Win us with honest trifles, to betray's
In deepest consequence.
*(Banquo)*


This supernatural soliciting
Cannot be ill, cannot be good. If ill,
Why hath it given me earnest of success,
Commencing in a truth?
*(Macbeth)*

---

**Activity 3**

1. Read the key quotations above. Pick out the words that appear to contrast with one another.

2. Re-read Macbeth's soliloquy from Act 1, Scene 3. How does Shakespeare's use of language suggest that Macbeth is already contemplating murdering Duncan?

# Act 1, Scene 4

At Duncan's court, Malcolm reports the execution of the former Thane of Cawdor, who died repenting his **'treasons'**. Duncan thanks Macbeth and Banquo for their selfless courage in battle, and then announces that his eldest son Malcolm will succeed him as the next king. Macbeth sets off to inform his wife that the king is going to honour them with a royal visit, confessing in an aside to his own **'black and deep desires'**.

- Having admitted that **'There's no art/ To find the mind's construction in the face'**, Shakespeare shows how Duncan is once more deceived by a Thane of Cawdor, describing Macbeth as **'a peerless kinsman'**.

- The simplicity of Banquo's pledge of loyalty to the king is contrasted with Macbeth's more **fulsome**, yet insincere, words.

- When Duncan proclaims Malcolm as his successor, he destroys Macbeth's hope that **'If chance will have me king, why chance may crown me/ Without my stir.'** *(Act 1, Scene 3)*

---

**Key quotations**

Duncan:    [...] Noble Banquo,
That hast no less deserv'd, nor must be known
No less to have done so, let me enfold thee
And hold thee to my heart.

Banquo:    There if I grow,
The harvest is your own.

---

**Activity 4**

Explore the different ways in which Shakespeare has contrasted Macbeth and Banquo in the play so far. You could draw up a table with two columns like the one below to record your ideas.

| Macbeth | Banquo |
|---|---|
|  |  |
|  |  |
|  |  |

**fulsome** flattering or gushing

**soliloquy** where a character voices aloud their innermost thoughts for the audience to hear

# Act 1, Scene 5

Lady Macbeth reads her husband's letter about the Witches. She is exhilarated by the prospect of Macbeth being king but fears that Macbeth does not possess the **'illness'** to **'wrongly win'** the crown.

She calls up diabolical forces to fill her with **'direst cruelty'** and prepare her for the task ahead. She greets Macbeth's return with joy and delight, and immediately takes control over planning the murder, which she calls **'This night's great business'**.

Lady Macbeth reads her husband's letter.

- Lady Macbeth's first thought is that the crown must be obtained by 'foul' means. She is not to be a force for good.

- By calling up evil spirits to her aid, **'unsex me here'**, and by viewing murder as **'great business'**, Lady Macbeth associates herself with the Witches and their dark powers.

- Lady Macbeth controls her husband with ease as she instructs him to assume the appearance of innocence.

---

**Key quotations**

>      Come, you spirits
> That tend on mortal thoughts, unsex me here
> And fill me from the crown to the toe topfull
> Of direst cruelty;
> *(Lady Macbeth)*

> Your face, my thane, is as a book where men
> May read strange matters. To beguile the time,
> Look like the time, bear welcome in your eye,
> Your hand, your tongue; look like th'innocent flower,
> But be the serpent under't.
> *(Lady Macbeth)*

---

## Activity 5

Appearances are deceptive in *Macbeth*.

1. Re-read what you have read of Act 1 so far and pick out all the uses of the words 'seem', 'seems', 'appears', 'face' and any other words that imply insincerity, disguise or attempting to deceive others.

2. Choose three quotations and explain *how* they suggest deception.

## Act 1, Scene 6

Duncan arrives at Macbeth's **'pleasant'** castle and is greeted cordially by Lady Macbeth. Duncan tells her of his high regard for Macbeth, whom he promises to favour.

- Banquo refers to the **'temple-haunting martlet'**, a little bird that often nests in the eaves of churches or where **'The air is delicate'**. This is clearly **ironic** as the castle soon turns into a **'hell-gate'** *(Act 2, Scene 3)*.
- Lady Macbeth follows her own advice by appearing to be innocent and loyal.

## Act 1, Scene 7

Alone, Macbeth contemplates the act of murder as well as its possible consequences. Just as he decides that his only motive for the killing is ambition, Lady Macbeth enters. Dismayed by Macbeth's decision not to go through with the murder, Lady Macbeth tries to change his mind, accusing him of being both cowardly and unloving.

- Macbeth's soliloquy reveals that, unlike Lady Macbeth, he is acutely aware of the implications of killing a king.
- Macbeth finds three reasons why he should not proceed: fear of retaliation – **'we but teach/ Bloody instructions'**; personal loyalty/duty to protect Duncan – **'He's here in double trust'**; Duncan's virtue and faultless kingship – **'this Duncan/ Hath borne his faculties so meek, hath been/ So clear in his great office'**.
- Lady Macbeth's successful **harangue** of her husband displays an unfeminine cruelty as she talks of her willingness to have **'dash'd the brains out'** of her baby.

> **harangue** an angry, critical attack on someone
>
> **irony** a literary technique where the intended meaning differs from what is said or presented directly

---

**Key quotations**

Macbeth:      Prithee, peace.
I dare do all that may become a man;
Who dares do more is none.

Lady Macbeth: What beast was't then
That made you break this enterprise to me?
When you durst do it, then you were a man.

---

**Activity 6**

Working in pairs, act out the conversation between Macbeth and Lady Macbeth to bring out their differing attitudes. Discuss whether Macbeth should sound impatient with his wife or if he should be pleading. Could Lady Macbeth play her lines as if she is hurt and upset rather than angry?

## Act 2, Scene 1

On his way to commit the murder, Macbeth meets Banquo and his son Fleance. Banquo delivers Duncan's **'unusual pleasure'** at the Macbeths' hospitality and also the gift of a diamond from Duncan for Lady Macbeth. When Banquo speaks of the **'the three weïrd sisters'**, Macbeth untruthfully claims not to think about them. Banquo makes it clear that he will not be involved in anything dishonourable.

Left alone, Macbeth sees a **'vision'** of a dagger leading him towards Duncan's chamber. This supernatural **manifestation** unsettles Macbeth, but he steels himself and exits to perform **'the bloody business'**.

- Shakespeare continues to contrast Macbeth and Banquo through their reactions to the Witches' prophecies.

- Macbeth's hallucination of **'a dagger of the mind'** could be caused by his conscience or could be further evidence that supernatural powers are at work.

- Macbeth's newfound courage and determination to kill Duncan are reflected in his references to **'murder'**, to the fierce **'wolf'** and to the cruel Roman tyrant, Tarquin.

Macbeth is unsettled by the vision of a dagger

---

**Key quotations**

Is this a dagger which I see before me,
The handle toward my hand? Come, let me clutch thee:
I have thee not, and yet I see thee still.
Art thou not, fatal vision, sensible
To feeling as to sight? Or art thou but
A dagger of the mind, a false creation,
Proceeding from the heat-oppressed brain?
(Macbeth)

How would you present the dagger to the audience if you were directing this scene? Is it the product of Macbeth's imagination or could the Witches be behind it? What will it look like on stage?

**manifestation** the appearance of a ghost, spirit or supernatural event

## Act 2, Scene 2

Lady Macbeth waits anxiously for news of Macbeth's **'success'**. Macbeth appears in a troubled state, unable to utter the blessing **'Amen'**, and also hearing voices.

Lady Macbeth is horrified that Macbeth has brought the evidence of the daggers with him and refuses to return to the murder scene. When she hears **'knocking/ At the south entry'**, she takes charge again, urging Macbeth to put on his nightgown and confidently stating, **'A little water clears us of this deed.'**

- Lady Macbeth's admission that **'Had he not resembled/ My father as he slept, I had done't'** suggests that she does have some sentimental feelings left.
- The irony of her suggestion that murder is **'easy'**, because the blood can be washed away, will be fully revealed in her sleepwalking actions in Act 5, Scene 1.
- There are signs of the beginnings of Macbeth's mental disintegration as he reports hearing voices crying **'Sleep no more'**. These could be the promptings of conscience or be part of the torment that the Witches inflict upon him. His final **couplet** contrasts strongly with the ending of the previous scene.

**couplet** two lines of verse, usually rhyming

**Activity 8**

Re-read Lady Macbeth's soliloquy at the beginning of Act 2, Scene 2. How does she reveal that she is not quite as fearless as she pretends?

## Act 2, Scene 3

The knocking rouses the Porter, who addresses the audience directly, asking them to imagine that he is the Porter of **'hell-gate'**. He opens the gate to Macduff and Lennox, who have called to escort Duncan on his way. Macbeth appears more collected than when we last saw him, although his brief replies to his fellow nobles suggest that he is nervous about what is about to be discovered.

Macduff's announcement of Duncan's murder, and the ringing of the 'the alarum bell', rouses the household. Macbeth explains why he has killed the 'murderers', prompting Lady Macbeth to draw attention away from her husband by appearing to faint. In the commotion, Duncan's sons Malcolm and Donaldbain resolve to flee to avoid being killed themselves. Banquo takes charge and proposes a meeting to 'question this most bloody piece of work/ To know it further'. He calls upon the protection of God in the fight against 'treasonous malice'.

- The Porter's reference to the castle as hell is ironic given what took place within its walls in the night.
- Macbeth uses his 'false face' *(Act 1, Scene 7)* throughout this scene.
- The fact that Duncan's sons flee to escape the 'daggers in men's smiles' throws suspicion of the murder on them. However, Banquo alone knows that Macbeth, as well as Malcolm, was likely to profit from the death of Duncan.

**Key quotations**

Who's there in th'other devil's name? Faith, here's an equivocator that could swear in both the scales against either scale, who committed treason enough for God's sake, yet could not equivocate to heaven. *(Porter)*

**Activity 9**

1. Why do you think Shakespeare decided to introduce the comical character of the Porter at this particular point in the play?

2. Discuss the significance of the Porter's reference to an equivocator at this point in the play.

## Act 2, Scene 4

Ross and an Old Man discuss the exceptional events in nature that occurred on the 'sore night' that Duncan was murdered. Ross concludes that 'the heavens' are 'troubled with man's act'. Macduff arrives and explains that Duncan's sons are suspected of having bribed the grooms to kill their father; therefore the kingship is to go to Macbeth. Macduff chooses not to go to Macbeth's coronation.

- The 'revolt' in nature on the night that Duncan was murdered suggests the seriousness of Macbeth's deed, which disrupted the natural order of things – a frequent idea in the play.
- Macduff's refusal to attend Macbeth's investiture will have dire consequences for his family.

**Activity 10**

Do you think the events described in the key quotation above are meant to represent Macbeth's unworthiness to gain the throne? Look at the other examples of unnatural occurrences in this scene and see if you can see parallels between the human world and non-human world of nature.

**Tips for assessment**

When writing about Duncan's murder and Macbeth's accession in your assessment, make sure you support your ideas with examples of the disruptions in nature that seem to echo the disruption in the state.

## Act 3, Scene 1

Banquo considers the Witches' prophecies and is suspicious that Macbeth **'played'st most foully'** for the kingship. Macbeth, although still outwardly friendly towards Banquo and urging him warmly to **'Fail not our feast'**, is secretly plotting to have him and his son killed.

- The audience will be shocked to see how Macbeth, no longer being coerced by his wife, continues to use violence to try to keep the crown.

**Key quotations**

    To be thus is nothing,
But to be safely thus. Our fears in Banquo
Stick deep, and in his royalty of nature
Reigns that which would be fear'd. 'Tis much he dares,
And to that dauntless temper of his mind,
He hath a wisdom that doth guide his valour
To act in safety.
(Macbeth)

**Activity 11**

What characteristics of the new king Macbeth does Shakespeare reveal in this scene?

**a)** Re-read Macbeth's soliloquy from Act 3, Scene 1. What characteristics are revealed in this speech? Do you see a change coming over Macbeth?

**b)** Now read Macbeth's conversation with the Murderers. Note that the beginning of the section with the Murderers is in **prose** rather than **verse**. What is the effect of this?

**c)** What kind of kingship is emerging here? Compare it with Duncan's.

**prose** any writing in continuous form without rhythm or rhyme

**verse** a group or series of groups of written lines, containing a rhythm or rhyme

## Act 3, Scene 2

Like her husband, Lady Macbeth is also finding her new status not quite as satisfying as she had hoped, especially as she can see that Macbeth is troubled. Macbeth reveals the extent of his mental state to his wife; he is suffering from **'terrible dreams'** linked with the idea that he has **'murder'd sleep'**.

- The opening lines of Lady Macbeth's soliloquy echo Macbeth's thoughts.
- The fact that Macbeth does not tell his wife what his plans for his enemies are, beyond promising **'A deed of dreadful note'**, shows the relationship between the couple to be deteriorating.

**Key quotations**

> Nought's had, all's spent
> Where our desire is got without content.
> 'Tis safer to be that which we destroy
> Than by destruction dwell in doubtful joy.
> *(Lady Macbeth)*

**Activity 12**

Re-read this scene between the couple aloud and make a note of all the images you can find relating to deceit, nature and sleep. Discuss why these are important in the play.

## Act 3, Scene 3

The hired Murderers wait for their victims to appear and are joined by a Third Murderer who replies **'Macbeth'** to their question, **'But who did bid thee join with us?'** Between them they murder Banquo, but Fleance escapes.

- This is the first murder that Shakespeare shows the audience. The onstage violence will now escalate as Macbeth becomes more hardened to shedding innocent blood.

### Activity 13

In some productions, the Third Murderer is played by one of the witches and sometimes by Ross. Explain how you would cast the role and what effect you would hope to achieve through your interpretation of who the third murderer is.

In this production, the Ghost of Banquo is physically present on stage

## Act 3, Scene 4

Macbeth and Lady Macbeth welcome their guests to the state banquet. The First Murderer brings Macbeth the news of Banquo's death and Fleance's escape. Although troubled by the news, Macbeth attempts to be cheerful for his guests. As he jokingly complains about Banquo's absence at the feast, Macbeth is horrified to see the Ghost of Banquo sitting at the table.

In his terror, Macbeth's makes an incriminating speech to the ghost. Lady Macbeth swiftly takes charge of the situation, explaining Macbeth's strange behaviour – talking to thin air and quaking with fear – as the result of a childhood infirmity, a passing fit. She tries to reason with him, but Macbeth's hallucination will not go away and since he **'grows worse and worse'** Lady Macbeth breaks up the banquet and sends the guests away.

Macbeth decides to take action against Macduff, who has insulted him by not attending the banquet, but also to consult further with the Witches.

- The apparition of Banquo's Ghost, like the imaginary dagger and the voices that he hears, may imply Macbeth's conscience manifesting itself in hallucination; alternatively, each 'supernatural' event might be attributed to the Witches.

- This is the last occasion where we see Lady Macbeth attempt to take control over her husband; here, he is unresponsive to her.
- Macbeth's conclusion, **'We are yet but young in deed'** is ominous as he plans more violence and speaks of his intention to return to the weird sisters to learn **'the worst'**.

---

**Key quotations**

    **I am in blood**
**Stepp'd in so far that should I wade no more,**
**Returning were as tedious as go o'er.**
**Strange things I have in head that will to hand,**
**Which must be acted ere they may be scann'd.**
*(Macbeth)*

---

**Activity 14**

Macbeth is famous for its many references to blood and gore. Count the number of times the words 'blood', 'bloody' or 'gory' appear in this scene and be on the lookout for such references in the rest of the play. Why do you think Shakespeare chose to use these words so frequently?

# Act 3, Scene 5

In the previous scene, Macbeth spoke of his intention to revisit the Witches. In this scene, Hecate chides the Witches for their involvement with Macbeth.

- The Witches' intention to **'draw him on to his confusion'** shows how Macbeth is being deceived by the Witches.

# Act 3, Scene 6

Lennox implies to another Lord that Macbeth was responsible for the deaths of Duncan and Banquo. In return, the Lord tells Lennox about the opposition to Macbeth centred on the English court where both Malcolm and Macduff have fled.

- The audience is explicitly asked to compare **'The gracious Duncan'** and **'the right-valiant Banquo'** with Macbeth, described as **'a hand accurs'd'**.

---

**Tips for assessment**

*Upgrade*

In your assessment, you may refer to the division of the play into three phases; Acts 1 and 2 show Macbeth gaining the crown, Act 3 shows the nature of his kingship, while Acts 4 and 5 show Macbeth's overthrow.

## Act 4, Scene 1

The Witches prepare a cauldron full of sickening ingredients. They agree to answer Macbeth's questions and offer to show him their **'masters'**. Macbeth receives three prophecies: that he must beware of Macduff; that he is invincible against any man born of woman; and that he will never be vanquished until Birnam Wood comes to Dunsinane.

Macbeth is reassured, but still insists on asking the question that most troubles him: **'shall Banquo's issue ever/ Reign in this kingdom?'** The Witches reveal **'a show of eight kings'** and the final image is of Banquo's Ghost, **'blood-bolter'd'**, as it appeared at the banquet. Lennox tells Macbeth that Macduff has fled to England.

- The Witches' prophecies offer false hope to Macbeth.
- The **'Horrible sight'** of Banquo's sons inheriting his crown dismays Macbeth.
- News of Macduff's flight causes Macbeth to decide to annihilate Macduff's family.

> **Key quotations**
>
> The castle of Macduff I will surprise;
> Seize upon Fife; give to th'edge o'th'sword
> His wife, his babes, and all unfortunate souls
> That trace him in his line. No boasting like a fool;
> This deed I'll do before this purpose cool,
> But no more sights.
> *(Macbeth)*

**issue** the collective term for children or descendants

**Activity 15**

Why do you think Macbeth reacts like this to his second experience with the Witches?

## Act 4, Scene 2

Ross and Lady Macduff discuss Macduff's flight to England. Though Lady Macduff complains that she has been abandoned, Ross defends her husband's wisdom. After Ross leaves, a messenger warns Lady Macduff to leave quickly, **'Hence with your little ones.'** Before she can act on his advice, murderers arrive, killing her little boy before attacking her.

- Macbeth's savagery is seen to be increasing as murderers kill a small boy on stage.
- Lady Macduff and her son talk about what it is to be a traitor before the murderers arrive – a key theme in the play.

# Act 4, Scene 3

In the English court, Malcolm tests Macduff's loyalty by claiming to be an immoral man. He lists his vices and Macduff declares him, **'Fit to govern?/ No, not to live.'** This reassures Malcolm that Macduff is not one of Macbeth's men sent to trap him.

As the two men discuss the **'sanctity'** of the English king Edward the Confessor and begin to plan the attack upon Macbeth, Ross arrives with news about the murder of Macduff's family. Macduff swears to kill Macbeth himself.

Malcolm's feigned confession to being full of vice is another example of a **'False face'** *(Act 1, Scene 7)*. However, Malcolm's motives are good as he is only testing Macduff's sincerity.

As Macduff struggles to understand Ross' terrible news, Malcolm instructs him to **'Dispute it like a man'**, reminding the audience of the importance of manhood as a theme in the play.

---

**Key quotations**

Malcolm:   **Dispute it like a man.**

Macduff:   **I shall do so;**
           **But I must also feel it as a man;**
           **[…]**

Malcolm:   **Be this the whetstone of your sword, let grief**
           **Convert to anger. Blunt not the heart, enrage it.**

Macduff:   **O, I could play the woman with mine eyes**
           **And braggart with my tongue. But gentle heavens,**
           **Cut short all intermission. Front to front**
           **Bring thou this fiend of Scotland and myself;**
           **Within my sword's length set him. If he scape,**
           **Heaven forgive him too.**

---

**Activity 16**

1. Discuss the significance of the key quotation above.

2. Re-read Act 4, Scene 3 from the entry of Ross to the end of the scene. What does Shakespeare want us to feel about Macduff and Malcolm here?

3. Consider the role of Ross in this scene and the previous scene. Discuss the dramatic effect that might be created by playing Ross as one of Macbeth's spies, as some directors have chosen to interpret him.

## Act 5, Scene 1

Lady Macbeth's Gentlewoman and her Doctor observe Lady Macbeth sleepwalking. She tries to rub her hands clean, crying **'Out, damned spot! Out, I say!'**, and re-enacts the exchange she had with Macbeth after he had killed Duncan. Her references to Banquo and to Lady Macduff also reveal her guilt. The Doctor believes, from her speech and actions, that she has been involved in murder.

Lady Macbeth as she sleepwalks

- There are several ironies here as Lady Macbeth echoes some of her own words spoken earlier in the play when she was fearless of the consequences of her actions.

- The Doctor appears to know that Lady Macbeth is in a suicidal state of mind: **'Remove from her the means of all annoyance'**.

### Activity 17

Re-read the whole of Lady Macbeth's sleepwalking scene and pick out the references to earlier speeches or events. What effect does Shakespeare create in this scene through his use of these echoes?

## Act 5, Scene 2

The remainder of Act 5 switches to the battlefield and the focus shifts between the Scottish and English forces marching together to defeat Macbeth. This scene focuses on the Scottish rebels who are marching on Macbeth's stronghold at Dunsinane.

Lennox, who has now turned against the king, discusses Macbeth with other rebel lords. Angus comments on the fact that even Macbeth's followers **'move only in command'** and do not love him.

- This is further proof of the worthlessness of his kingship, which commands no loyalty.

## Act 5, Scene 3

The action returns to Macbeth's castle, where Macbeth reminds himself of the Witches' prophecy that he cannot be overthrown by one **'born of woman'** or until Birnam Wood **'remove to Dunsinane'**. He tells the Doctor to cure Lady Macbeth.

- The news that 10,000 soldiers approach does not dismay Macbeth but he reflects upon what his kingship has robbed him of: **'honour, love, obedience, troops of friends'**.
- Macbeth links Lady Macbeth's illness to the **'sick'** state of the country.

**Activity 18**

Macbeth's moods seem to be constantly changing in this scene as he steels himself for battle and reflects on his life. Create a graph, charting his mood swings from the beginning to the end of the scene.

## Act 5, Scene 4

Malcolm, having reached Birnam Wood, instructs his soldiers to **'hew him down a bough'** which will be used as camouflage for their advance. The wood begins to **'move'**.

- We see how the Witches' prophecies used equivocation to lull Macbeth into a sense of false security.

## Act 5, Scene 5

Back in Dunsinane, Macbeth is confident of victory. Then he hears a **'cry of women'** and learns that Lady Macbeth is dead. This prompts one of the most famous soliloquies in Shakespeare, summing up the **futility** of life. A Messenger reports the advance of Birnam Wood.

- The death of Lady Macbeth makes Macbeth reflect on life and how meaningless it seems.
- Macbeth is shocked to hear of the **'moving grove'** advancing towards Dunsinane and he begins to **'doubt th'equivocation of the fiend/ That lies like truth'**, echoing Banquo's warning in Act 1, Scene 3.

**Key quotations**

Tomorrow, and tomorrow, and tomorrow,
Creeps in this petty pace from day to day
To the last syllable of recorded time;
And all our yesterdays have lighted fools
The way to dusty death. Out, out, brief candle,
Life's but a walking shadow, a poor player
That struts and frets his hour upon the stage
And then is heard no more. It is a tale
Told by an idiot, full of sound and fury
Signifying nothing.
*(Macbeth)*

**Activity 19**

Look closely at Macbeth's speech on the previous page and compare it with the tone of his opening and concluding speeches in this scene and his first speech in Scene 3. What is Shakespeare intending to convey here?

## Act 5, Scene 6

This brief scene shows Malcolm's army arrive at Dunsinane and battle commences.

- It is significant that Malcolm and Macduff, who have both suffered much at Macbeth's hands, lead the assault.
- Macduff anticipates the battle and the **'blood and death'** to come.

## Act 5, Scene 7

Macbeth kills Young Siward, who taunted him with the title of **'abhorred tyrant'**. Macduff prepares to engage in combat with Macbeth to avenge the death of his family.

- Macbeth's body count rises as he scorns Young Siward for having been **'born of woman'**.

## Act 5, Scene 8

The **climax** of the play occurs as Macbeth and Macduff come face to face. As they fight, Macbeth boasts of his **'charmed life which must not yield/ To one of woman born'** only to be told that **'Macduff was from his mother's womb/ Untimely ripp'd'**, revealing that Macduff was not born in the normal way, but by caesarean section. This disclosure almost makes Macbeth give up but, faced with the prospect of yielding to Malcolm, Macbeth recovers some of his courage and fights on. Macduff kills him and leaves the stage with his body.

- Macbeth is finally faced with the truth about the prophecies, realizing that he has been misled by the Witches.

**Key quotations**

And be these juggling fiends no more believ'd
That palter with us in a double sense,
That keep the word of promise to our ear
And break it to our hope.
*(Macbeth)*

**Activity 20**

Look at the key quotation to the left. How has Shakespeare made this 'realization' inevitable throughout the play for the audience?

**climax** the highest or most intense part of the play or a turning-point in the action

**futility** pointlessness

## Act 5, Scene 9

Macduff displays Macbeth's decapitated head and pronounces Malcolm king of Scotland. Malcolm thanks all who have fought for him.

- In a measured speech, and much in the manner of the gracious Duncan, Malcolm honours them with new titles, **'Henceforth be earls'**, and promises to restore order and harmony to Scotland.

- The rightful king is on the throne – a happy ending.

**Activity 21**

Why do you think Shakespeare has broken the last section of the play into eight relatively short scenes? What effect does this create?

Macduff challenges Macbeth to combat

# Structure

*Macbeth* is one of Shakespeare's major tragedies. For the structure of the action in the play, Shakespeare was influenced by two theatrical models from previous centuries:

- Senecan tragedy (1st century AD)
- the morality play (15th and 16th centuries).

## Senecan tragedy

Seneca was a Roman philosopher, and poet and adviser to the Emperor Nero. He wrote nine plays based on Greek drama and its themes. His bloodthirsty plots, peppered with ghosts and witches, inspired numerous Jacobean tragedies.

Seneca's theatrical debt to classical Greek tragedy is immense. Not only did he adopt plots and themes from Greek drama but he also adopted the narrative structure of the plays, which traditionally depict the fall of a great man, the **protagonist**, from prosperity to misery and death, because of the individual's **tragic flaw**.

To be truly tragic, the suffering of the hero must have wider implications, affecting the whole state. The tragic hero traditionally experiences complications, suffering setbacks and **reversals** of fortune in his life, which build to a dramatic climax before ending in **catastrophe.** At this point the hero experiences a **tragic recognition** of his circumstances, causing the audience to experience a **catharsis** or 'purging' of pity and fear.

It is unlikely that Shakespeare had access to the texts of the classical dramatists – Aeschylus, Sophocles and Euripides – who inspired Seneca. Shakespeare's familiarity with the classical Greek tragic form comes from his knowledge of Seneca's plays.

In terms of dramatic structure, however, Seneca departed from classical models and was the first to introduce the five-act structure that is used in Macbeth and which was widely adopted by **Renaissance** playwrights.

Other features that Shakespeare borrowed from Senecan tragedy include:

- focus on '*scelus*' or crime – Macbeth is one of the first 'criminal heroes' in English tragedy
- preoccupation with violent deaths
- exploration of the powers of the supernatural – the Witches, the Ghost of Banquo
- presence of vaulting ambition as a character trait
- use of philosophical/rhetorical speech: some of the key speeches in *Macbeth* bear striking similarities to specific speeches from Seneca's tragedies.

---

**catastrophe** in Greek tragedy, the concluding part of the play where the protagonist accepts ruin

**catharsis** in Greek tragedy, an outrush of audience emotion; pity for the ruined hero and fear for their own fate

**protagonist** the main character

**Renaissance** the revival of classical styles of art and literature in Europe in the 14th–16th centuries

**reversal (*peripeteia*)** a reversal of fortunes

**tragic flaw (*hamartia*)** a character fault that leads to the protagonist's downfall

**tragic recognition (*anagnorisis*)** recognition of the error of one's ways

---

In this 2013 production at the Globe Theatre, directed by Eve Best, the Witches appear rather like classical Vice figures

## The morality play

Morality plays were popular in late medieval England. They presented moral instruction through the experiences of an Everyman figure, who met abstract characters, such as Vice, Virtue, Pleasure and Valour, on his spiritual journey towards **salvation** or **damnation**.

It is possible to see some vestiges of this traditional drama form in *Macbeth* as the play is very much about Macbeth's spiritual journey towards damnation. Macbeth is beset by Vice figures, including the Witches and Lady Macbeth, who tempt him to his own harm. Virtue can be seen in Duncan, Banquo and in Lady Macduff; Valour can be seen in Macduff and Malcolm. The entrance to Macbeth's castle at Dunsinane is compared with **'hell-gate'** by the Porter character, who has much in common with the familiar Trickster or diabolical character from the morality play tradition.

Shakespeare borrows from, but does not slavishly adopt, the conventions of these influential models to create a unique tragedy of the individual, Macbeth.

## Number and arrangement of scenes in *Macbeth*

There are 29 individual scenes of varying lengths, arranged into five acts. *Macbeth* is one of Shakespeare's shortest plays and has no subplot.

Acts 1 and 2 introduce the main action: Macbeth is inspired to gain the crown through killing the king. This is accomplished by Act 2, Scene 3 and its immediate consequence – the crowning of Macbeth – is discussed in the closing scene of Act 2.

Structurally, we have the **exposition** in Act 1 and the development in Act 2. Macbeth has achieved his goal. The first and second acts are sometimes referred to as the rising action.

In Act 3 we see Macbeth, as king, beginning to face complications: Macduff has not attended his investiture; Banquo may suspect him as Duncan's murderer; and Malcolm and Donaldbain are abroad, free to turn against him. Macbeth's relationship with his wife is deteriorating as he plans new murders without involving her.

Fleance's escape and Banquo's 'appearance' at the banquet, as a **'blood-bolter'd'** *(Act 4, Scene 1)* ghost, causes Macbeth to return to the Witches, hardening his heart to perform more atrocities. This might be said to be the climax of the play.

Act 4 shows a reversal in Macbeth's fortunes as the Witches confirm that Banquo's issue will produce a line of kings. He also receives the prophecies that cause him to think himself invincible. We see Macbeth descend to his lowest moral point when he decides to slaughter Macduff's innocent family. There is also a reversal in that we see the forces of good coming together against Macbeth, when Malcolm and Macduff join forces with the English to oust **'this fiend of Scotland'** *(Act 4, Scene 3)*.

Act 5 completes the reversal and presents Macbeth's decline; his wife kills herself and he concludes that he has **'liv'd long enough'** *(Act 5, Scene 3)*. Catastrophe strikes when Macduff reveals that he was not **'born of woman'** and Macbeth achieves tragic recognition as he sees that he has been duped by the Witches. He has traded his immortal soul for a brief and unhappy reign as king. The audience feel pity for Macbeth and fear for themselves and their own souls. In the final scene, order is restored to the troubled state. The last two acts are sometimes described as comprising the falling action.

---

**damnation** the belief in Christian teaching that the souls of sinners and criminals will be damned after death and burn in hell for eternity

**exposition** key information to help the audience make sense of the action and characters in the play

**salvation** the belief in Christian teaching that good souls will go to heaven to be saved and live with God for ever

---

## Time

Shakespeare's play is based on historical characters. The real Macbeth (1005–1057) reigned for 17 years (from 1040) before he was killed in battle by Malcolm (not Macduff). The time frame that Shakespeare adopts appears to be much shorter. Although Macbeth refers to **'old age'** in Act 5, Scene 3, the events that the play depicts appear to happen in rapid succession and this is emphasized by the use of very short scenes in Act 5.

**Activity 22**

Work out a timeline for the following key events in the play using days, months and years. Refer to the text to justify your decisions.

- Defeat of the Norwegians/rebels
- Macbeth and Banquo meet the Witches
- Macbeth and Banquo receive thanks from the king
- Duncan's murder
- Macbeth's investiture
- Banquo's murder
- Macbeth revisits the Witches
- Slaughter of the Macduff family
- Macduff meets with Malcolm in England
- The march on Scotland
- Macbeth is killed

Compare and discuss your timeline with others in your class.

## Place

In the 29 scenes of the play, the action takes place in a range of different locations, both indoors and outdoors. Elizabethan and Jacobean drama was performed in the late afternoon on an open stage; there was no lighting and no scenery as such, although the actors used occasional furniture and props to signify specific locations. Playwrights had to convey the necessary details of individual settings through words alone. For example, when Duncan arrives at Macbeth's castle, Shakespeare presents the exterior of the castle through the exchange between Duncan and Banquo, beginning **'This castle hath a pleasant seat'** *(Act 1, Scene 6).*

**Activity 23**

Look again at the beginning of selected scenes to see how Shakespeare suggests the location of the setting in the characters' dialogue.

## Patterns in the plot

Shakespeare uses a variety of patterns in the play, for example, *Macbeth* begins and ends on the battlefield. In Act 1, Macbeth is victorious in defeating the rebels and enemy forces on behalf of his king; in Act 5, it is Macbeth who is killed as a traitor to Scotland, a **regicide** and a **usurper**.

In the play, two kings are killed: the gracious King Duncan and the **'butcher'** *(Act 5,*

Scene 9) King Macbeth. Two wives die: the nurturing and loving mother Lady Macduff, and the **'fiend-like'** *(Act 5, Scene 9)* and unnatural queen Lady Macbeth.

There are two meetings between Macbeth and the Witches. In the first, Macbeth and Banquo both receive prophecies, but each deals with his supernatural visitation in a different way.

Two courts are depicted: the court of Macbeth, where courtiers are fearful and murderers seem free to visit, and the court of the English King Edward the Confessor, where Malcolm finds a safe haven and subjects receive blessings from their king.

> **regicide** a king-killer
>
> **usurper** someone who seizes the crown without the right to do so

### Activity 24

How many other examples can you find of Shakespeare using pairs to help to structure the events in the play?

## Writing about structure

*Upgrade*

In your assessment, you will never be asked merely to recount the plot of *Macbeth*, but you may be asked to comment on its structure or on the ordering of events in the play. Think about the different effects that Shakespeare achieves by, for example, placing one particular scene after another.

In Act 4, for example, Macbeth ends the first scene brooding about Macduff's escape to England, deciding to **'give to th'edge o'th'sword/ His wife, his babes, and all unfortunate souls/ That trace him in his line'** *(Act 4, Scene 1)*. As the next scene opens with Lady Macduff and her little boy talking to Ross, the audience will be tense with anticipation having just heard Macbeth promise to have these innocents slaughtered. Look for other examples of this type of effect and be prepared to write about them in the exam.

# Biography of William Shakespeare

It is thought that Shakespeare (1564–1616) wrote *Macbeth* between 1605 and 1606

- Although he is considered by many to be one of the world's most significant writers, relatively little is known about William Shakespeare. What is known has been gleaned from various legal and church documents that have survived from Elizabethan times and from what other writers of the period wrote about him.

- Shakespeare was born in Stratford-upon-Avon, probably on 23 April 1564. His father John Shakespeare was a glove-maker and leather merchant who became the high bailiff of Stratford (a position equivalent to Lord Mayor) during William's early childhood. Shakespeare probably attended the grammar school in Stratford-upon-Avon.

- The next documented event in Shakespeare's life is his marriage to Anne Hathaway in 1582. Their first daughter Susanna was born in 1583. The couple later had twins, Hamnet and Judith. Hamnet died in childhood at the age of 11 in 1596.

- After the birth of his twins, William Shakespeare disappears from all records until 1592. This period is regularly referred to as his 'Lost Years'.

- Shakespeare began to establish himself as an actor and playwright in London and, by 1594, he was not only acting and writing for the Lord Chamberlain's Men (called the King's Men after the ascension of James I in 1603), but was a managing partner in the business as well.

- Shakespeare was a prolific and popular playwright and poet, writing 37 plays and a sequence of sonnets as well as two longer poems, 'Venus and Adonis' and 'The Rape of Lucrece'. Shakespeare's plays are usually divided into the following types: Tragedies, Comedies, Histories, late Romances.

- In addition, Shakespeare owned shares in both the theatrical company and the Globe Theatre, which brought great financial benefits; in 1597, Shakespeare bought one of the largest houses in Stratford for his retirement. He died in 1616.

## Activity 1

See how many of Shakespeare's plays you can name. Put each of the plays into one of the following categories:

- Tragedy
- Comedy
- History
- Romance.

# Historical and cultural context

## Historical context

Shakespeare wrote *Macbeth* between 1605 and 1606, shortly after the death of Elizabeth I and the ascension of King James of Scotland to the English throne. At this time Shakespeare's theatre company, the Lord Chamberlain's Men, was renamed the King's Men and it performed regularly at court for private audiences, including for the king.

It is likely that Shakespeare wrote *Macbeth* with this most important audience member – the king – in mind. Not only does the play deal with King James' direct ancestors (one of whom was Banquo), but it also explores witchcraft, a theme of particular interest to James who had published his own ideas about witches in a text entitled *Daemonologie* in 1597.

The play also considers the issue of 'just' kingship as well as the threat of regicide. James faced two assassination attempts himself. The first, in 1600, when he was king of Scotland but not yet of England, was mounted by the Earl of Gowrie and his brother. The second, on 5 November 1605, was the famous 'Gunpowder Plot'. This plot was hatched by a group of Catholics opposed to the Protestant king and outraged by harsh new legislation against them. The plot targeted King James, the royal family and dozens of government officials. It was foiled when Guy Fawkes, one of the conspirators, was discovered in the Palace of Whitehall with large quantities of gunpowder. The other conspirators were rounded up, tried in court, convicted of treason and executed on 30 January 1606.

In *Macbeth*, allusions to the Gunpowder Plot occur when the Porter refers to one of his imaginary visitors **'knocking'** on the door as **'an equivocator'** *(Act 2, Scene 3)*. Shakespeare seems to be making an in-joke by referring to a priest named Father Garnet, who was arrested for his part in the Gunpowder Plot, but under oath during the trial used 'equivocation' in his testimony to try to avoid the death penalty. The play's original audience would immediately have understood this line as a mockery of the Catholics' perceived practice of equivocation.

> **Key quotations**
>
> Faith, here's an equivocator that could swear in both the scales against either scale, who committed treason enough for God's sake, yet could not equivocate to heaven. *(Porter, Act 2, Scene 3)*

## Sources

As with many of his plays, Shakespeare drew inspiration for the plot for *Macbeth* from historical sources, using, in particular, Raphael Holinshed's authoritative *Chronicles of England, Scotland, and Ireland* (1577). Shakespeare combined different stories about the history of the kings of Scotland to create his unique story.

The *Chronicles* include an account of the reign of King Malcolm II, whose throne passed first to Duncan I in 1034 and then to Macbeth in 1040; both were Malcolm's grandsons. However, Shakespeare turned to the story of King Duff's murder (967) by one of his servants Donwald in his portrayal of Duncan's bloody slaughter.

### The real Macbeth

The historical character Macbeth had a very good claim to the throne both through his own grandfather, Malcolm II, and by marriage to the granddaughter of a king of Scotland. In the play, it is suggested that Macbeth was chosen by his peers to succeed Duncan.

## Contemporary attitudes towards witchcraft and the supernatural

Medieval Scotland, in common with many other European states, believed in witches and in their ability to make prophecies and to control human affairs. Witchcraft was generally regarded as an evil practice, which depended upon a relationship with the Devil, and as a threat to social stability. King James himself contended that witchcraft was a reality and that those who dabbled in it should be punished.

### Activity 2

Find out all you can about attitudes towards witches, their powers and limitations in the Jacobean period.

## Contemporary attitudes towards religion

Religion was a complicated issue in Tudor and Stuart society. The great Tudor king Henry VIII began to move away from Catholicism when he declared himself head of the Church in England in 1534. His son Edward VI's reign saw a continuation of the movement towards Protestantism. Shakespeare was writing first under a Protestant Queen – Elizabeth I – and then under her successor, the Protestant King James I. However, there were still significant numbers of English and Scottish Catholic families and churchmen who refused to give up their Catholic faith. Some of these were persecuted for their beliefs in the 16th and 17th centuries.

For the purposes of understanding the religious context of *Macbeth*, it is enough to appreciate that all Shakespeare's audiences would have believed in the very real existence of heaven and hell. The crimes that Macbeth commits against his king, his peers and against innocent women and children would be seen as mortal sins and a guarantee that his soul would end up in hell.

## The Great Chain of Being

Shakespeare's audience would also have believed in the Great Chain of Being, which was a concept of a natural order put in place by God in which every creature and element in nature had its proper place within the 'chain'. The chain began with God at the top of a hierarchy, which descended through angels, saints, kings and nobles and then down through the ranks of ordinary human beings to the lowliest peasant and beyond to animals, which were also ranked from the highest – the lion – to the lowest – spiders and worms. Beneath animals and birds came trees and plants and beneath them, rocks and minerals.

It was believed that provided this natural order was preserved, the state would operate harmoniously, but if it was disturbed, for example, as when Macbeth killed the king, the chain was broken and the state would erupt into chaos.

## The divine right of kings

Linked to belief in the Great Chain of Being was the belief that the king was appointed to rule on Earth by God and was God's representative on Earth. Therefore, when Macbeth murders King Duncan, he has committed a crime against God himself.

The Great Chain of Being represents a hierarchical order of the world, with God at the top

# Theatrical context

## Elizabethan and Jacobean theatres

Shakespeare was writing at a time when drama was flourishing in London. Theatre had become one of the most popular forms of entertainment towards the end of the 16th century, as performances that had previously been held in the courtyards of inns or in the houses of noblemen moved into purpose-built theatre buildings. The first London theatre was built at Shoreditch in 1576; the owner was James Burbage who named it The Theatre.

When the 21-year lease for the ground upon which The Theatre had been built was due to expire, at the end of 1597, Burbage decided to dismantle the building and transport the timberto a new site on Bankside in Southwark, where his new theatre, called the Globe Theatre, was built by carpenter Peter Smith.

The Globe Theatre was one of various Elizabethan theatres that opened on Bankside, outside the city limits after plays and theatres were banned in the City of London.

The Globe Theatre was certainly the most magnificent theatre in London. Other London theatres built towards the end of the 16th century included the Curtain, the Rose and the Fortune. The Globe Theatre was home to the company that Shakespeare belonged to, the Lord Chamberlain's Men, and it was owned by a syndicate, made up of the landowner, James Burbage's two sons Richard and Cuthbert, and five acting members of the Chamberlain's Men, one of whom was Shakespeare. As a shareholder, Shakespeare was entitled to 10% of the profits of the theatre, which is thought to have contributed to the foundation of Shakespeare's personal wealth.

## Shakespeare's contemporary dramatists

With the proliferation of purpose-built theatres came a similar surge in the number of educated men who turned to writing for the theatre, tempted by the prospect of financial reward. These writers included Thomas Kyd, Christopher Marlowe, George Chapman, Ben Jonson, John Lyly and Thomas Middleton.

Most playwrights began their careers as actors attached to one or other of the numerous acting companies. Then, after an apprenticeship in the theatre, they began writing their own work as well as adapting or rewriting the works of others. As there was no such thing as dramatic copyright in the 16th century, many playwrights avoided having their plays published for fear of rival companies **plagiarizing** their work and profiting from their hard work.

**plagiarism** the illegal copying of someone else's work; a form of literary theft

### Writing about theatrical context

*Upgrade*

It is important to be aware if your assessment requires explicit reference to the context of *Macbeth*. If context is required, the examiner will not be simply looking for dates or unrelated historical facts. Instead, try to explain how the context gives you greater insight into the play and how it can be interpreted in a way that is relevant to the question you are answering.

You may include references to the original staging arrangements in Jacobean theatres if you are writing about the play in production in your assessment tasks. Further information about context is provided in the performance section.

# Main characters

## Macbeth

Macbeth is the play's protagonist and his character fits the profile of a tragic hero, being a great man, who falls because of his fatal flaw of ambition. He is initially presented as Duncan's **'valiant cousin'** *(Act 1, Scene 2)*; a brave defender of the realm and completely loyal to his king.

The apparently chance meeting with the Witches – that the audience see is pre-planned by them – changes all this. Shakespeare shows us how susceptible Macbeth is both to the apparently **'fair'** prophecies of the witches, as well as to the evidently **'foul'** manipulation of him by Lady Macbeth.

Between them, they prompt Macbeth's transformation from a courageous and reflective, yet ambitious, man to the tyrant, **'hell-hound'** and **'villain'** *(Act 5, Scene 8)* that Macduff accuses him of being before he defeats him in combat at the climax of the play.

Sean Bean as Macbeth in the 2002 production

One of the most significant aspects of the presentation of Macbeth is that he retains the sympathy of the audience in spite of the terrible things that he does. Shakespeare achieves this through giving the audience access to Macbeth's most private thoughts, either through Macbeth's dialogue with his wife or in soliloquy.

### Activity 1

**a)** Re-read Macbeth's speech from the section of Act 1, Scene 3 beginning, **'Two truths are told…'** to where his private thoughts end, **'Come what come may,/ Time and the hour runs through the roughest day.'** Using modern speech, write your own version of his reaction to the fact that the Witches' prophecies are coming true.

**b)** Go through the same process with Macbeth's soliloquy from the opening of Act 1, Scene 7, beginning, **'If it were done when 'tis done'.**

**c)** What do we learn about Macbeth's conscience at these points in the play?

Macbeth is not only a courageous soldier, he is also a husband and later in Act 1 we see him in a more domestic setting with his wife. Lady Macbeth has already decided that she is going to have to 'chastise' *(Act 1, Scene 5)* her husband into seizing the crown because she believes Macbeth to be 'too full o'th'milk of human kindness' *(Act 1, Scene 5)* to do wrong on his own initiative. Lady Macbeth's acknowledgement of her husband's good nature helps to create audience sympathy for Macbeth. We are horrified to see how she overpowers his better instincts and persuades him to kill Duncan.

Lady Macbeth uses different strategies to convince Macbeth to murder Duncan; she attacks his manhood and she accuses him of disloyalty to her. The bravery of her speeches rouses Macbeth's capacity for evil; appealing to the soldier in him, she presents the murder of a defenceless old man as a 'great quell' *(Act 1, Scene 7)* and, like the Witches, she persuades Macbeth that he cannot fail.

What Lady Macbeth does not predict, however, are the consequences of pressurizing Macbeth into committing murder, both for him and for her marriage.

Initially, Macbeth appears slightly unhinged by having 'done the deed' *(Act 2, Scene 2)*. He is unable to return to Duncan's chamber to replace the daggers; he begins to hear voices and immediately regrets his actions and recognizes that, through his actions, he has lost his true self.

**Key quotations**

I'll go no more.
I am afraid to think what I have done;
Look on't again, I dare not.
*(Macbeth, Act 2, Scene 2)*

To know my deed, 'twere best not know myself.
[*Knock within*]
Wake Duncan with thy knocking: I would thou couldst.
*(Macbeth, Act 2, Scene 2)*

Later, Macbeth becomes hardened to murderous acts. He murders Duncan's grooms in cold blood and appears to think little of murdering his once dear friend Banquo. He regrets the escape of Fleance and, in an act of sheer malice, has the entirely innocent family of Macduff slaughtered.

His kingship brings him little satisfaction. The knowledge that he has forfeited his immortal soul 'For Banquo's issue' *(Act 3, Scene 1)* torments him continually. However, the fact that he articulates his mental torment suggests that he still has a vestige of conscience left, despite his murderous actions, and the audience is never fully alienated from him.

As he becomes more distant from his queen, and as his noblemen begin to defect to support Malcolm's claim to the throne, Macbeth returns to consult the Witches, only to have his worst fears about Banquo's issue confirmed. He takes some comfort from the Witches' hollow assurances that **'none of woman born/ Shall harm Macbeth'** *(Act 4, Scene 1)* but his life has become meaningless to him. Even before he hears of the death of his wife, Macbeth admits to himself, **'I have liv'd long enough'** *(Act 5, Scene 3)*.

Macbeth's tragic recognition that life is **'a tale/ Told by an idiot'** *(Act 5, Scene 5)* is reinforced when he is confronted by Macduff and made to realize that he has been deceived by the Witches. He sees himself as a victim of **'these juggling fiends[...]/ That palter with us in a double sense'** *(Act 5, Scene 8)* but, rather than admit defeat, Macbeth regains some respect from the audience by choosing to **'try the last'** *(Act 5, Scene 8)*. The audience experiences the **'pity and fear'** intended in tragedy as we see the **'Th'usurper's cursed head'** *(Act 5, Scene 9)* for the last time and compare the remnant of Macbeth that we see before us with the fearless warrior in Act 1, fighting to defend his king and country.

## Activity 2

In groups of four, prepare a presentation on 'Who was to blame for Duncan's death?' Each group member should present the case for one of the following:

- the Witches
- Lady Macbeth
- Macbeth
- Duncan himself.

Macbeth's character is associated with themes of kingship, the supernatural, good and evil, honour and manhood, the imagination/conscience, appearance and reality, deceit/equivocation and ambition. Shakespeare also uses **motifs** of blood and clothing throughout the play, applied principally to Macbeth.

### Tips for assessment

Unlike a novelist, who can describe or comment upon characters to help the reader understand them, a playwright must convey each personality through dialogue or soliloquy. In your assessment, you'll need to show how Shakespeare presents his characters through what they say and how they say it, as well as through their actions and through the spoken opinions of others.

## Lady Macbeth

A painting by Gertrude Demain Hammond of Lady Macbeth

Lady Macbeth's first appearance is quite disturbing. As she reads Macbeth's letter about the Witches' prophecies, we see a woman who is prepared to go to any lengths to see her husband crowned as king. Although she is thrilled by Macbeth's news, Lady Macbeth concludes that without her 'spirits' to ignite his ambition, Macbeth's good nature will prevent him from seizing the crown unlawfully.

Lady Macbeth's willingness to associate herself with diabolical spirits; to 'unsex' herself, to be filled with cruelty and to be utterly excluded from feelings of remorse makes for a chilling audience experience.

When she learns that Duncan is visiting the castle for the night, her immediate response is to plan to murder him. Lady Macbeth takes over from where the Witches left off in stirring Macbeth to kill the king. She instructs Macbeth on how to behave, dismisses his qualms and insists on taking over 'This night's great business' (Act 1, Scene 5).

The audience watch Lady Macbeth welcome the gracious Duncan to her home in Act 1, Scene 6, where her behaviour exactly matches her advice to her husband to 'bear welcome in your eye,/ Your hand, your tongue; look like th' innocent flower/ But be the serpent, under't.' (Act 1, Scene 5).

motif a word, phrase or image in literature that is repeated to create specific effects

remorse a feeling of regret and repentance for having done something wrong

When Macbeth, having wrestled with his conscience, announces that 'We will proceed no further in this business' (Act 1, Scene 7), Lady Macbeth is horrified. She accuses her husband of being less than a man and goads him into agreeing to go through with the murder.

> **Key quotations**
>
> When you durst do it, then you were a man.
> And to be more than what you were, you would
> Be so much more the man. Nor time, nor place
> Did then adhere, and yet you would make both.
> They have made themselves and that their fitness now
> Does unmake you. I have given suck and know
> How tender 'tis to love the babe that milks me:
> I would, while it was smiling in my face,
> Have pluck'd my nipple from his boneless gums
> And dash'd the brains out, had I so sworn
> As you have done to this.
> *(Lady Macbeth, Act 1, Scene 7)*

**Activity 3**

Shakespeare does not tell us what has happened to the Macbeths' child, but one favoured theory is that the child died. How might this 'fact' affect the way Lady Macbeth delivers the above speech? How will it affect the way Macbeth reacts? In pairs, act out the exchanges between Lady Macbeth and her husband in Act 1, Scene 7.

Although Lady Macbeth does not physically carry out the murder of the king, claiming in soliloquy that she would have been quite capable of doing so had Duncan not 'resembled/ My father as he slept' *(Act 2, Scene 2)*, she is just as guilty as Macbeth of regicide. She plans the murder, returns the bloody daggers to the chamber to implicate the grooms and effectively stage-manages the cover-up. Shocked to find Macbeth so traumatized by his deed, she urges him to bed, reassuring him ironically that 'A little water clears us of this deed' *(Act 2, Scene 2)*.

No sooner has Macbeth been crowned than Lady Macbeth's influence over him begins to wane. He turns away from her and plans his own further murders to try to ensure that the Witches' prophecies about Banquo's line will not be fulfilled. Like her husband, Lady Macbeth finds little pleasure in the ill-gotten crown and, though she begs Macbeth to stop brooding about the murder, telling him 'what's done, is done' *(Act 3, Scene 2)*, she is not content.

Lady Macbeth comes to Macbeth's rescue once more in the banquet scene in Act 3, Scene 4 when she tries to make light of his terrified reaction to Banquo's Ghost. As Macbeth comes close to revealing his guilt, questioning his guests about their ability to look calmly on such sights while his cheeks are 'blanch'd with fear' *(Act 3, Scene 4)*, Lady Macbeth takes control and dismisses the assembled nobles swiftly, blaming Macbeth's strange behaviour on an invented childhood infirmity and telling them to go. It is her last appearance in her right mind.

Lady Macbeth appears, sleepwalking, in the first scene of Act 5. The audience see how Macbeth's deed in murdering Duncan has not only led to the 'murder of sleep' for himself but also for Lady Macbeth, who can get no rest as she relives the events of the night of the murder over and over again. Only in this scene does the audience begin to pity her as she reveals that, despite her invocation to the spirits in Act 1, she is not immune from remorse after all.

When Macbeth hears of her death later, he does not even have time to mourn her as he prepares to repel Malcolm's army.

Lady Macbeth is associated with themes of the supernatural, deceit, ambition, sleep, manhood and womanhood. She is contrasted with Lady Macduff, who is shown to be a pattern of femininity and motherhood. Many of Lady Macbeth's early utterances turn out to be ironic and she is also linked with the motif of blood.

## Banquo

Shakespeare uses Banquo as a **foil** to Macbeth. The Witches meet both men as they return from battle in Act 1. While Macbeth is inspired by their prophecies to murder the king, Banquo appears unaffected by their prediction that he will father a line of kings.

When the Witches' first prediction comes true, Banquo warns his friend of the dangers of being enkindled 'unto the crown/ Besides the Thane of Cawdor' (Act 1, Scene 3).

> **foil** a character whose function is to serve as a contrast to another character

---

**Key quotations**

But 'tis strange,
And oftentimes, to win us to our harm,
The instruments of darkness tell us truths;
Win us with honest trifles, to betray's
In deepest consequence.
(Banquo, Act 1, Scene 3)

---

Although the above quotation shows that he anticipates exactly what will happen to Macbeth, Banquo does not appreciate the danger that he is in himself. Before Macbeth kills Duncan, he meets Banquo on his way to bed and subtly sounds him out by appearing to offer him further 'honour' if he supports him in the future. However, Banquo's response is direct and honourable.

> So I lose none
> In seeking to augment it, but still keep
> My bosom franchis'd and allegiance clear,
> I shall be counsell'd.
> *(Banquo, Act 2, Scene 1)*

Banquo's honour is a challenge to Macbeth. He fears, correctly, that Banquo may suspect him as the murderer of Duncan and he resents his superior qualities. Despite being king, Macbeth does not feel secure while Banquo lives.

**Key quotations**

> Our fears in Banquo
> Stick deep, and in his royalty of nature
> Reigns that which would be fear'd. 'Tis much he dares,
> And to that dauntless temper of his mind,
> He hath a wisdom that doth guide his valour
> To act in safety. There is none but he,
> Whose being I do fear;
> *(Macbeth, Act 3, Scene 1)*

Banquo becomes Macbeth's next victim. While still showing him the false face of friendship, calling him 'our chief guest' *(Act 3, Scene 1)* and telling him how he values his 'good advice' *(Act 3, Scene 1)*, Macbeth hires murderers to kill Banquo and his son as they return to the castle for the banquet. The irony is that Banquo keeps his promise to go to the feast and appears in ghostly form at the banquet to unsettle Macbeth and break up the celebration. Banquo's final appearance is also as a ghost in the apparition scene *(Act 4, Scene 1)*, when he taunts Macbeth, smilingly, with the vision of his lines of kings.

Banquo is linked to the themes of good and evil, honour and manhood, kingship and bravery.

Banquo's Ghost appears

## Duncan

Although Duncan appears relatively briefly in the play, his character is very important. As a good and gracious king who recognizes and rewards the loyalty of his thanes, Duncan is a foil to Macbeth, whose reign brings only terror and insecurity both to his noble peers and to Scotland generally.

If Duncan has a fault, it is to be too trusting, the very opposite of Macbeth who sees danger and threats to his power all around him. Duncan is full of praise for Macbeth and Banquo, whose valour has defeated the enemy.

In victory, Duncan's first instinct is to confer honour and a new title on Macbeth and to promise **'signs of nobleness'** for **'all deservers'** *(Act 1, Scene 4)*. His announcement that Malcolm is created the Prince of Cumberland and named as successor to his throne seals Duncan's fate. He repeats his mistake of putting his absolute trust in the Thane of Cawdor, placing himself in mortal danger by honouring Macbeth with a kingly visit to his home.

We do not see Duncan again after he is welcomed to Dunsinane by Lady Macbeth. However, we hear about his good qualities, helping to reinforce the audience's impression of a just and gracious king who, only hours before he is slaughtered in his sleep at Lady Macbeth's insistence, sends a diamond to thank her for her hospitality.

Duncan is associated with the themes of kingship, appearance and reality, good and evil. He is also vividly associated with the motif of blood.

**Key quotations**

> Besides, this Duncan
> Hath borne his faculties so meek, hath been
> So clear in his great office, that his virtues
> Will plead like angels, trumpet-tongu'd, against
> The deep damnation of his taking-off.
> *(Macbeth, Act 1, Scene 7)*

# Malcolm

Malcolm is yet another foil to Macbeth but, unlike Duncan and Banquo, he escapes Macbeth's violent clutches and returns to claim the throne that was promised him in Act 1.

Shakespeare presents him as a worthy successor to Duncan. In the early part of the play, Malcolm speaks warmly of the Sergeant who saves him and he reports the execution of the first Thane of Cawdor fairly and without malice. He is sensible enough to take flight after the discovery of Duncan's murder, recognizing, with his brother Donaldbain, that the safest way to avoid being the next target of the killer is to **'shift away'** *(Act 2, Scene 3)*.

We next see Malcolm in the English court, where Macduff seeks him out to persuade him to return to Scotland. Malcolm mistrusts Macduff's motives and believes he may be one of Macbeth's spies, so he tests Macduff by accusing himself of having numerous vices and none of the qualities necessary to be a good king. Macduff's despair at this point persuades Malcolm of his sincerity and they conspire together to overthrow the tyrant Macbeth.

Shakespeare ensures that we see the parallel between Duncan and Malcolm, and Malcolm's great contrast to Macbeth; in the final scene of the play we see Malcolm promising to reward all his supporters and to re-establish order and harmony in Scotland.

Malcolm is associated with the themes of good and evil, kingship and harmony/chaos.

# Macduff

Macduff is Macbeth's **nemesis**. He discovers Duncan's dead body in Act 2, Scene 3 and challenges Macbeth with **'Wherefore did you so?'** when Macbeth declares that he has killed the grooms.

Suspicious of Macbeth, Macduff does not attend the coronation nor does he accept Macbeth's invitation to the banquet, which is taken as a personal insult by the new king.

Once Banquo is killed, Shakespeare uses Macduff (and Malcolm) to represent the forces of good ranged against the evil reign of Macbeth, so that, although we see little of him, we hear about his whereabouts and intentions. For example, Macduff is described by Ross in Act 4, Scene 2 as **'noble, wise, judicious, and best knows/ The fits o'th'season.'**

He joins forces with Malcolm in raising an army against Macbeth and turns out to be the one man **'of no woman born'** *(Act 5, Scene 8)* who can conquer the otherwise invincible tyrant.

> **nemesis** in Greek tragedy, a person or force that inflicts punishment or revenge

**Activity 6**

Go through the play looking for references to Macduff. Make a list of what is said about him by others; this is one of the key methods that Shakespeare uses to build up a clear picture of Macduff.

Shakespeare creates a thrilling moment of theatre as the great adversaries, Macbeth and Macduff, face one another to battle to the death.

> **Key quotations**
>
> Macbeth:  I bear a charmed life which must not yield
>          To one of woman born.
>
> Macduff:  Despair thy charm;
>          And let the angel whom thou still hast serv'd
>          Tell thee, Macduff was from his mother's womb
>          Untimely ripp'd.
>
> *(Act 5, Scene 8)*

Macduff kills Macbeth in mortal combat, not for his own gain but to restore Scotland to its rightful king. However, in killing the **'butcher'** himself, he gains revenge for the deaths of his family.

Macduff is associated with themes of equivocation, good and evil, loyalty/treachery, and manhood.

**Tips for assessment**

If you are asked about good and evil in your assessment, remember to write about the four good men – Banquo, Duncan, Malcolm and Macduff – in the play who help to counterbalance the evil in Macbeth.

## The Witches

The Witches seem to thrive in darkness and bad weather; thunder announces each of their appearances, giving them an ominous presence. Their riddling pronouncement that, **'Fair is foul, and foul is fair'** *(Act 1, Scene 1)* acts as a key to the events that follow where, as Macbeth comments after their first prediction has come true, **'nothing is,/ But what is not.'** *(Act 1, Scene 3)*

The Witches' equivocation betrays Macbeth into believing that he is invincible. However, they cannot be blamed for inciting Macbeth to murder Duncan and Banquo, or to have Macduff's family murdered. They may have awakened Macbeth's inner evil but they do not create it, nor do they urge him to do ill as Lady Macbeth does.

On each occasion when the Witches appear, Shakespeare shows them interacting with one another before Macbeth appears. This suggests that they are real people and not, as some commentators suggest, merely projections of Macbeth's fevered imagination, as the 'air-drawn dagger' *(Act 3, Scene 4)* could be. Banquo also sees them in Act 1, Scene 3 and neither Macbeth nor Banquo appear to be especially shocked by how they look, only by their sudden appearance and disappearance and by their seeming ability to foretell the future.

**Activity 7**

In groups of three, go through the text finding references to the Witches. How would you present them? Act out the opening scene of the play, using different ideas about how they might appear.

There have been many conflicting suggestions made about who or what the Witches are. We need to remember that Shakespeare, when writing the play:

- knew of King James' interest in witches
- found reference to Macbeth's encounter with witches in his source material, where it was reported simply that he and Banquo 'met them three women in strange and wild apparel'. Later in the *Chronicles*, these women are referred to as 'weird sisters'. There is also a reference to Macbeth having learned to be wary of Macduff from 'certain wizards'.

The Witches are, nevertheless, very important characters. At first they seem to be casting spells and doing magic at a fairly low level – killing pigs for spells, harassing a woman for not sharing her chestnuts, creating a storm at sea – but once Macbeth has met them, he can never forget what they have promised. And once he has gained the crown, he is especially concerned about their predictions for Banquo.

Initially, the Witches seek out Macbeth; but as he becomes deeper and deeper steeped in blood, he voluntarily seeks them out to find out **'By the worst means, the worst'** *(Act 3, Scene 4)* what fate holds in store for him.

The Witches are associated with themes of appearance and reality, good and evil, equivocation, and the supernatural.

# Minor characters

## Lady Macduff

Lady Macduff only appears in one scene but she is not an insignificant character. She acts as a foil to Lady Macbeth by being an emblem of gentle motherhood.

When she is warned by a messenger about the approaching 'danger' and advised to go 'Hence with your little ones' *(Act 4, Scene 2)*, her reply reveals her to be Shakespeare's representative of feminine goodness and innocence in the play.

> Whither should I fly?
> I have done no harm. But I remember now
> I am in this earthly world where to do harm
> Is often laudable, to do good sometime
> Accounted dangerous folly. Why then, alas,
> Do I put up that womanly defence,
> To say I have done no harm?
> *(Lady Macduff, Act 4, Scene 2)*

Lady Macduff is associated with the themes of good and evil, love, womanhood, loyalty/betrayal. Her little boy, killed in front of her, also represents innocence slaughtered by Macbeth's regime.

## Other thanes, nobles and courtiers

Shakespeare creates a sense of Macbeth's court through the inclusion of a range of thanes, nobles and courtiers. They often act as messengers or they offer opinions about Macbeth, Malcolm or others, serving to show how national feeling turns against Macbeth as his actions become more blatantly violent and unkingly.

Of these characters, the most prominent are Ross and Lennox. Ross has a steady presence throughout the play but his character is never precisely defined. Some directors, both in stage and film versions of the play, have interpreted Ross as a self-serving character, who sides with whoever is most likely to advance him. We first meet him reporting Macbeth's bravery to Duncan in Act 1, Scene 2; he is the one chosen to tell Macbeth of his new title, Thane of Cawdor.

Ross appears in the scene immediately following the discovery of Duncan's body; unlike Macduff, Ross chooses to attend Macbeth's coronation. In the banquet scene, Ross criticizes Banquo for not turning up, perhaps appearing eager to criticize one of his fellow nobles and ingratiate himself with the new king.

In Act 4, Ross visits Lady Macduff to tell her of Macduff's flight to England, but he doesn't stay long enough to protect her from the murderers. He reports the deaths of Macduff's family to Macduff in the English court. In the play's last scene, we see he has positioned himself in the winning camp once more, lending his voice to hail the new king of Scotland.

## Activity 8

Look carefully at all of Ross's appearances and speeches. Do you think there is enough evidence to suggest that Ross is yet another 'false face'?

In some versions of the play, Ross appears as the Third Murderer of Banquo and/or he is part of the group of thugs who murder Macduff's family.

Lennox, Mentieth, Angus and Caithness have less prominent roles to play. They act either as plot devices (e.g. when Lennox informs Macbeth of Macduff's flight to England) or they are simple commentators on the action, filling in plot details for the audience in a narrative rather than a dramatic way.

## Activity 9

1. In groups of four, read aloud Act 5, Scene 2. The characters who appear are Menteith, Caithness, Angus and Lennox, and none of them is a developed character. What is the purpose of this scene?

2. All characters have a purpose however small their roles. Working in your group, divide up the following characters between you and write a sentence explaining what each role contributes to the play: Fleance, the Porter, the 'bloody' Sergeant, Hecate, Donaldbain, Seyton, the Doctor, the Gentlewoman, the Murderers, Old Siward, Young Siward, Old Man, Apparitions.

## Writing about characters

*Upgrade*

In your assessment you may be asked to write about one or more characters. Equally important is considering how Shakespeare presents the character and how he uses the character to communicate his ideas to an audience.

Always try to refer to the following, where applicable:

- what the character looks or sounds like (if stated in the play)
- what the character says about himself/herself and about others
- what others say about the character
- contrasts and comparisons with other characters
- what the character does – his/her actions and/or reactions in the play
- the language the character uses when speaking.

When thinking about the purpose or function of the character, you should consider the following possible uses:

- to give/receive information
- to develop the plot
- to act as a foil or contrast to other characters
- to alter the mood or atmosphere, e.g. to add humour or pathos
- to act as a **catalyst**, bringing about change in the story.

**catalyst** an agent of change

## Character map

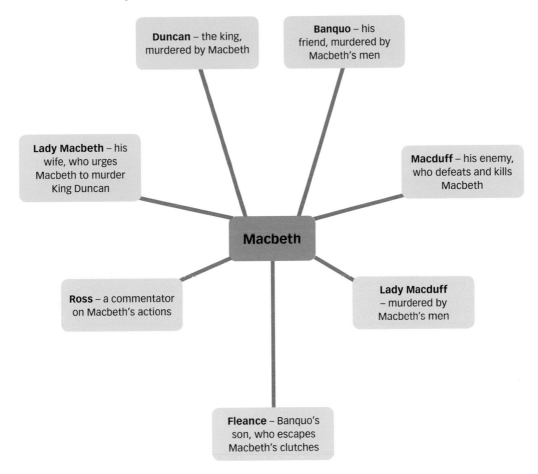

**Duncan** – the king, murdered by Macbeth

**Banquo** – his friend, murdered by Macbeth's men

**Lady Macbeth** – his wife, who urges Macbeth to murder King Duncan

**Macduff** – his enemy, who defeats and kills Macbeth

**Macbeth**

**Ross** – a commentator on Macbeth's actions

**Lady Macduff** – murdered by Macbeth's men

**Fleance** – Banquo's son, who escapes Macbeth's clutches

# Stage directions

Shakespeare wrote his plays to be performed by his own acting company so he did not need to include very many precise stage directions. He didn't prepare the texts for publication himself either; they were published by others after his death. These conditions probably account for the fact that there are so few stage directions in his plays. In the copy of *Macbeth* that you are studying, there are probably a few stage directions, at the beginning of each scene and throughout individual scenes, indicating the location or setting of the scene and the entrances and exits of various characters. However, these have probably been supplied by the editor of your edition of the play rather than by Shakespeare.

## Edited editions

An edition is a printed version of a text that has been prepared for publication, not by the original author, but by an editor, who is responsible for overseeing the accuracy of the edition. Sometimes, editors also supply helpful background information as well as explaining the meanings of individual words and phrases.

Shakespeare included within the characters' lines, all the essential information that he wanted to convey. So, for example, in Act 1, Scene 3, the fact that Macbeth says to the Witches, **'Say [...] why/ Upon this blasted heath you stop our way'** tells us that the scene is set on a heath. Similarly, Act 2, Scene 1 begins by establishing the time:

*Enter* Banquo, *and* Fleance, *with a Torch-bearer before him*

BANQUO:  How goes the night, boy?

FLEANCE:  The moon is down; I have not heard the clock.

BANQUO:  And she goes down at twelve.

FLEANCE:  I take't, 'tis later, sir.

## Activity 1

Look at the characters' dialogue or monologues at the beginning of selected scenes to see how Shakespeare suggests the time of day or night that the scene takes place.

In the 1971 film *The Tragedy of Macbeth* the director Roman Polanski set some scenes in a landscape like Scottish heathland

Other stage directions include the division of the play into acts and scenes. Often these divisions are blurred when we are watching the action unfold in the theatre, as characters exit and enter in rapid succession. When we are reading the play, however, these divisions are useful in keeping track of the development of the plot.

**Speech, dialogue and monologue**

Dialogue occurs between characters when they are speaking to one another. A monologue or soliloquy is a term for the speech of a character who is speaking alone, or who speaks for a long time without interruption. A duologue is a section of text where two characters talk directly to one another.

# Verse, prose and rhyme

Shakespeare's use of language is very distinctive; his use of verse and of **imagery** are part of what makes Shakespeare's plays unique.

Shakespeare writes mainly in **blank verse** and he uses a form called **iambic pentameter**. This is a poetic **metre** that consists of ten syllables per line, with five of them stressed for emphasis. Look at the following lines, from the beginning of Act 4, where Macbeth is demanding that the Witches tell him what he wants to know:

I <u>con</u>jure <u>you</u> by <u>that</u> which <u>you</u> pro<u>fess</u>,
Howe'er you <u>come</u> to <u>know</u> it, <u>an</u>swer <u>me</u>.
*(Act 4, Scene 1)*

Here, the stresses are underlined.

**Activity 2**

In pairs, try reading the above lines aloud, first putting emphasis on the syllables underlined and then on the other syllables. What is the effect of rejecting Shakespeare's intended rhythm?

**blank verse** poetry that does not rhyme

**iambic pentameter** a line of verse with ten syllables, where the stress falls on the second syllable (and then every other syllable) in the line, e.g. 'di dum' as in: **Throw <u>phys</u>ic <u>to</u> the <u>dogs</u>, I'll <u>none</u> of <u>it</u>**. *(Act 5, Scene 3)*

**imagery** visually descriptive or figurative language

**metre** the rhythm of lines of verse, dependent on the number of syllables in a line and the stress pattern

Shakespeare uses blank verse in a flexible way throughout the play and you will notice that characters are able to have quite natural sounding conversations with one another, still using blank verse.

> **Key quotations**
>
> Macbeth:   Your children shall be kings.
>
> Banquo:                                         You shall be king.
>
> Macbeth:   And Thane of Cawdor too: went it not so?
>
> Banquo:     To th'selfsame tune and words who's here?
> *(Act 1, Scene 3)*

Sometimes, Shakespeare uses a device called **stichomythia** to create tension. In the above example, Macbeth and Banquo also share a single line of iambic pentameter, creating a more naturalistic effect.

> **Key quotations**
>
> Macbeth:           I have done the deed. Didst thou not hear a noise?
>
> Lady Macbeth:   I heard the owl scream and the crickets cry.
>                             Did not you speak?
>
> Macbeth:           When?
>
> Lady Macbeth:   Now.
>
> Macbeth:           As I descended?
>
> Lady Macbeth:   Ay.
>
> Macbeth:           Hark, who lies i'th'second chamber?
>
> Lady Macbeth:   Donaldbain.
> *(Act 2, Scene 2)*

For the most part, the lines do not rhyme with one another, although Shakespeare often ends a scene with a **rhyming couplet**, which he uses to sum up the closing mood of the scene, as here, at the end of Act 2, Scene 1, where Macbeth has steeled himself to kill Duncan:

*A bell rings*

I go, and it is done. The bell invites me.
Hear it not, Duncan, for it is a knell
That summons thee to heaven or to hell.
*(Act 2, Scene 1)*

Notice how the use of short phrases within the metrical line suggests that Macbeth is pausing as he contemplates the deed to come. The first line disrupts our expectation of iambic pentameter by having 11 syllables; this may possibly be intended to suggest Macbeth's disturbed state of mind.

Shakespeare uses shorter lines and continuous rhyming couplets in his presentation of the Witches. This helps to create an other-worldly aspect to the characters. Probably one of the most famous of all Shakespeare's rhyming couplets is the Witches' chant as they await their second meeting with Macbeth:

**Double, double toil and trouble;**
**Fire burn, and cauldron bubble.**
*(Act 4, Scene 1)*

The metre of the Witches' lines in the quotation above is called trochaic tetrameter and is made up of four feet of **trochees**. A trochee is made up of one stressed syllable followed by an unstressed one. This reversing of the stress creates a distinctive and persistent rhythm to the Witches' speeches, which are both shorter and sound faster than the iambic pentameter spoken by nobility in the play.

It is conventional in most of Shakespeare's plays to find that the royal and noble characters speak in blank verse, whereas prose is spoken by lower ranking and/or comic characters. In *Macbeth* prose is used as follows:

- Lady Macbeth reading Macbeth's letter about meeting the Witches at the beginning of Act 1, Scene 5
- Macbeth's first exchanges with the Murderers in Act 3, Scene 1
- the Porter's speech in Act 2, Scene 3
- the exchange between Lady Macduff and her son before the arrival of the Murderers, in Act 4, Scene 2
- the majority of Lady Macbeth's sleepwalking scene in Act 5, Scene 1.

### Activity 3

Re-read each of the sections of the play listed above. Why do you think prose is appropriate in each case?

**rhyming couplet** when only two lines of poetry end in rhyme

**stichomythia** the rapid exchange of brief lines of dialogue

**trochee** poetic metre in which the stress falls on the first syllable (and then on every other syllable), e.g. 'dum, di' as in '<u>Thrice</u> the <u>brindled</u> <u>cat</u> hath <u>mew'd</u>.'
*(Act 4, Scene 1)*

# Figurative language

In Shakespeare's time, it was usual to refer to going to *hear* a play, rather than to *see* one. This was because of the importance of the **poetry** used in communicating the playwright's intentions; character is created through what individuals say *and do*, but atmosphere (like time and place) was created through words alone. *Macbeth* is a dark play full of violence, deceit and danger. Shakespeare creates this brooding darkness through his choice of vocabulary as well as through his use of imagery.

He also uses repetition as a device for emphasizing key themes and ideas throughout the play. For example, the word 'blood' is used over 40 times in the play; 'sleep' is referred to over 30 times. The word 'night' occurs nearly 50 times, while 'light' appears just over 20 times. These word statistics are not important in themselves, but the high incidence of these words helps to create the bleak atmosphere of the play. They become motifs that engage the audience's notice, guiding us to see Shakespeare's meaning more clearly.

Much of the language of the play draws its power from both natural and unnatural images, especially as Scotland hurtles towards chaos and disorder under Macbeth's rule.

> ### Activity 4
>
> **a)** Working in teams, select two or three scenes and see how many references you can find to the following natural occurrences: the elements (earth, fire, water, air), birds, animals, trees, rivers, seas, lakes, forests, heath.
>
> **b)** What effect do you think Shakespeare intended to create by making so many references to nature in this play?

**Figurative language** is language that is not literal. For example, in the banquet scene when Macbeth says to the First Murderer **'There's blood upon thy face'** *(Act 3, Scene 4)*, he is speaking literally – there is blood on his face. However, when Macbeth says to Lady Macbeth, later in the same scene:

> **I am in blood**
> **Stepp'd in so far that should I wade no more,**
> **Returning were as tedious as go o'er.**
> *(Act 3, Scene 4)*

He is using figurative language, as this is a **metaphor** that suggests the scale of Macbeth's bloody deed so far.

Other figurative language includes **similes**, where Shakespeare compares one thing to another (usually dissimilar) thing, using the word 'like' or 'as'. For example, in Act 1, Scene 7, Macbeth compares Duncan's virtues to **'angels'** to emphasize Duncan's purity.

Macbeth and Lady Macbeth after the killing of Duncan

**figurative language** language that uses figures of speech, is metaphorical and not literal

**metaphor** the use of a word or phrase in a way that is not literal, e.g. Duncan's planting/nurturing metaphor: **'I have begun to plant thee and will labour/ To make thee full of growing.'** *(Act 1, Scene 4)*

**poetry** a relatively short piece of literature where meaning is conveyed through imagery and expressed using a set rhythm or rhyme

**simile** a comparison of one thing with another, using 'as' or 'like', e.g. **'signs of nobleness like stars shall shine'** *(Act 1, Scene 4)*

### Activity 5

In pairs, re-read Act 1, Scene 7 aloud and pick out two further examples of the use of simile, two metaphors and two literal statements. Compare your selections with others in your group.

## Dominant recurrent images

In addition to repeating individual words such as 'blood' (41), 'chance' (9), 'fortune'/'fate' (7) and 'murder' (over 30), to name a small selection, Shakespeare also uses recurrent images in his plays that support the main themes.

In Macbeth, the dominant recurrent images and metaphors relate to clothing and to feasting. The first clothing images appear in Act 1 Scene 3, when Ross greets Macbeth with the title of Thane of Cawdor. Macbeth answers:

The Thane of Cawdor lives. Why do you dress me
In borrow'd robes?
*(Act 1, Scene 3)*

Banquo then continues this image, comparing Macbeth's new honour to new
clothes:

New honours come upon him
Like our strange garments, cleave not to their mould,
But with the aid of use.
*(Act 1, Scene 3)*

When Macbeth tries to justify his decision not to proceed with the murder plot to his
wife, he refers to his recently acquired title and to the opinions of his peers, using
clothing imagery:

He hath honour'd me of late, and I have bought
Golden opinions from all sorts of people,
Which would be worn now in their newest gloss,
Not cast aside so soon.
*(Act 1, Scene 7)*

In Act 2, Scene 4, Macduff wishes Ross will find things well done at Macbeth's
investiture, adding 'Lest our old robes sit easier than our new' and suggesting
that change may not be for the better.

As the play draws towards its end, Angus, one of the rebel thanes, describes
Macbeth's situation using clothing imagery to belittle the troubled king:

Now does he feel
his title
Hang loose about him,
like a giant's robe
Upon a dwarfish thief.
*(Act 5, Scene 2)*

To fully appreciate the
purpose of these images,
which suggest that
clothes somehow reflect
the inner man as well as
being able to mask him,
we need to try to imagine
a world where fashion
was not ever-changing
or throw-away as it is
today. And where feasting
was not such a common
occurrence either!

Patrick Stewart's
uniform in the
Rupert Goold film
of 2009 instantly
hints at Macbeth's
inner qualities and
his success as a
commander of
fighting men

Images of feasting and banqueting are used to suggest both spiritual nourishment and physical well-being. Duncan expresses his delight in Macbeth's loyalty in Act 1, Scene 4, saying, 'in his commendations I am fed;/ It is a banquet to me', while Banquo's absence at Macbeth's real banquet 'Lays blame' upon him *(Act 3, Scene 4)*. Macbeth's reaction to the 'cry of women' in Act 5, Scene 5 causes him to reflect on his 'diet' of murder; he says 'I have almost forgot the taste of fears; [...] I have supp'd full with horrors' *(Act 5, Scene 5)*.

> **Activity 6**
>
> **a)** See how many more references you can find to clothes/garments/robes in the play. Some references are literal and some are metaphorical.
>
> **b)** Next, look for references to food and drink, feasting and nourishment.
>
> **c)** What effects do you think Shakespeare was trying to achieve through these images?

A further set of recurrent images relates to babies, infants and children. This is perhaps unsurprising given that so much of Macbeth's discontent, having gained the crown, is that the fates have decreed that Banquo's children, and not Macbeth's, will inherit the kingship.

> **Key quotations**
>
> Upon my head they plac'd a fruitless crown
> And put a barren sceptre in my gripe,
> Thence to be wrench'd with an unlineal hand,
> No son of mine succeeding. If't be so,
> For Banquo's issue have I fil'd my mind;
> For them, the gracious Duncan have I murder'd,
> Put rancours in the vessel of my peace
> Only for them, and mine eternal jewel
> Given to the common enemy of man,
> To make them kings, the seeds of Banquo kings.
> *(Macbeth, Act 3, Scene 1)*

# Language and character

One of the ways that a playwright is able to create *distinct* characters in a play is to give them each a distinctive manner of speaking. To see how this works, you need to look at each character in turn and ask:

- What does he or she say?
- How does he or she say it?

We have seen that almost all the characters in the play speak in blank verse, which gives considerable conformity to the way they are presented. However, different characters tend to use different image clusters.

The frequently recurring references to 'blood' are most often used by Macbeth and Lady Macbeth, pointing to their willingness to shed blood to reach their goals.

Macbeth is the character who uses the most imagery related to the natural world, while Lady Macbeth also refers to nature and to the supernatural. Both refer frequently to night, to darkness and to sleep. Macbeth also refers frequently to haste and speed as the plot gathers momentum and hurtles towards his final catastrophe.

Duncan's language is notable by his frequent use of thanks and praise; he refers to planting – as Malcolm does in the closing speech of the play – suggesting his nurturing nature, tending to the growth and cultivation of the country as opposed to Macbeth's destruction of it.

**Key quotations**

| Character | Quotation | Motif/theme |
|---|---|---|
| Macbeth | Stars, hide your fires, <br> Let not light see my black and deep desires, <br> (*Act 1, Scene 4*) | Light/darkness |
| | Light thickens, <br> And the crow makes wing to th'rooky wood; <br> (*Act 3, Scene 2*) | Darkness and nature |
| | It will have blood they say: blood will have blood. <br> Stones have been known to move and trees to speak. <br> Augures, and understood relations, have <br> By maggot-pies, and choughs, and rooks brought forth <br> The secret'st man of blood. <br> (*Act 3, Scene 4*) | Blood and nature |
| Lady Macbeth | Come, thick night, <br> And pall thee in the dunnest smoke of hell, <br> That my keen knife see not the wound it makes, <br> Nor heaven peep through the blanket of the dark, <br> To cry, 'Hold, hold.' <br> (*Act 1, Scene 5*) | Darkness; heaven and hell |
| | [...] look like th'innocent flower, <br> But be the serpent under't. <br> (*Act 1, Scene 5*) | Natural world |
| | If he do bleed, <br> I'll gild the faces of the grooms withal, <br> For it must seem their guilt. <br> (*Act 2, Scene 2*) | Blood |

**Key quotations**

| Duncan | Welcome hither.<br>I have begun to plant thee and will labour<br>To make thee full of growing.<br>*(Act 1, Scene 4)* | Welcome/planting |
|---|---|---|
| Malcolm | My thanes and kinsmen,<br>Henceforth be earls, the first that ever Scotland<br>In such an honour nam'd. What's more to do<br>Which would be planted newly with the time,<br>As calling home our exil'd friends abroad<br>*(Act 5, Scene 9)* | Gratitude/honour/<br>planting |

**Activity 7**

Create your own table of quotations and add further quotations to support the patterns shown above. You should extend the table to include Banquo, Macduff, Lady Macduff and the Witches.

## Writing about language

*Upgrade*

An understanding of Shakespeare's use of language is vital when you are writing in assessments. Make sure that you have something to say about:

- Shakespeare's use of blank verse, rhyming couplets and prose
- the way he uses imagery throughout the play to create its dark and dangerous tone
- Shakespeare's use of repeated word clusters to distinguish between characters
- the way language supports the themes of the play
- Shakespeare's use of irony, especially in the speeches of Duncan and Lady Macbeth
- the use of equivocation and ambiguity.

We frequently refer to themes when we are discussing plays, novels and poems. Themes hold the key to the meaning of any piece of literature. They are the ideas that readers recognize as being significant as they engage with a writer's work. Themes are distinct from the content of a story or the plot of a play but they are not separate from them. Readers are able to develop a deeper understanding of a play or novel when they notice recurrent themes.

*Macbeth* is a highly political play. Its plotline follows the fortunes of a man who assassinates a king in order to gain the crown for himself. Many of the themes of the play help to underpin Shakespeare's exploration of the politics of his day. In turn, many modern directors use the play to explore 21st-century politics.

# Kingship

Kingship can be identified as a significant theme in *Macbeth* because the plot includes the murder of a good king, the rise and overthrow of a wicked king, and the succession of the rightful king in the closing moments of the play. Additionally, characters in *Macbeth* often discuss the qualities of good and bad kings quite explicitly, and the language and imagery within the play includes frequent reference to the **artefacts** of kingship such as the crown, sceptre and robes of state.

> **artefact** object or thing of cultural or historical interest

In *Macbeth* the word 'king' appears 18 times in Act 1 alone. The audience are first presented with a picture of the reigning King Duncan as he receives good news from the battlefield in Act 1, Scene 2. Then, immediately afterwards, in Scene 3, the Witches prophesy that Macbeth will be **'king, hereafter'** and that Banquo **'shalt get kings'**. These prophecies are the catalyst to all the ensuing action.

Shakespeare compares Macbeth's reign with that of Duncan's, showing us that while Duncan is a gracious and fair king, rewarding **'deservers'** *(Act 1, Scene 4)*, trusting his thanes (a little too much) and generously naming his successor, Macbeth operates a completely opposite kind of rule. Macbeth's kingship, achieved through the cowardly stabbing

The whole play is driven by Macbeth's obsession with becoming king and the consequences of that happening

of Duncan, begins with the murder of his closest friend and ends only after he has alienated his court, butchered the innocent family of Macduff and brought Scotland to the brink of ruin. In Shakespeare's time, it was believed that kings were appointed by God to rule as if as God's 'deputy' on earth; so to kill a king was the greatest crime that could be committed.

> **Key quotations**
>
> [...] each new morn,
> New widows howl, new orphans cry, new sorrows
> Strike heaven on the face, that it resounds
> As if it felt with Scotland and yell'd out
> Like syllable of dolour.
> *(Macduff, Act 4, Scene 3)*

The above speech, spoken to Malcolm in the English court, is intended to portray the state of Scotland under Macbeth's kingship. Later in the same scene, Malcolm lists the qualities of a good king: 'justice, verity, temp'rance, stableness,/ Bounty, perseverance, mercy, lowliness,/ Devotion, patience, courage, fortitude' *(Act 4, Scene 3)*. To highlight how far from the ideal king Macbeth is, in Act 4, Scene 3 we hear Malcolm commending the English king Edward the Confessor, in whose court he is living and who he describes as a 'good king' and one who 'solicits heaven' (rather than Witches) and who has 'a heavenly (rather than diabolical) gift of prophesy' and healing.

When Malcolm concludes the play, under the gaze of Macbeth's severed head, Shakespeare makes sure that Malcolm echoes the style of kingship that he has learned from his father Duncan, promising honours for all his loyal supporters and invoking the help of God to steer him in his forthcoming reign.

**Activity 1**

In pairs, try to find further references to kingship in the play. Also look out for other related ideas such as loyalty, allegiance, betrayal, treason and treachery.

# Manhood

Another important theme is what it is to be a man. We see this first in the scene where Lady Macbeth goads Macbeth into the murder of Duncan by belittling his manhood, telling him 'When you durst do it, then you were a man' *(Act 1, Scene 7)*.

Later, in the banquet scene (Act 3, Scene 4) she spits 'Are you a man?', as Macbeth looks on the Ghost of Banquo with horror, and demands 'What, quite unmanned in folly?'. Macbeth responds by telling her **'What man dare, I dare'** *(Act 3, Scene 4)*, reminding the audience briefly of the Captain's first description of **'brave Macbeth'** as he **'carv'd out his passage'** in battle *(Act 1, Scene 2)*, as he equates manhood with bravery.

For Macduff, manhood is a larger concept. When he hears of the slaughter of his wife and children, Macduff cries out in grief and Malcolm tells him to **'Dispute it like a man'** *(Act 4, Scene 3)*, which suggests that he finds Macduff's emotions womanly, but Macduff responds emphatically, saying, **'I shall do so;/ But I must also feel it as a man;/ I cannot but remember such things were/ That were most precious to me.'** *(Act 4, Scene 3)*

For Macduff, being a man is also about being a loving husband and father, not merely a strong, killing machine. This is important in helping the audience to applaud Macduff's victory over Macbeth in the closing scenes of the play.

Banquo's Ghost terrifies Macbeth

Elsewhere in the play, Shakespeare considers what it means to be a man as opposed to an animal and, in Macbeth's meetings with the Witches, being a man is more about being a mortal as opposed to a supernatural being.

**Activity 2**

1. Re-read the play to find as many examples as you can of references to 'man' or 'men'.

2. Now look how Shakespeare presents womanly qualities. Compare and contrast the presentation of Lady Macbeth and Lady Macduff. Do they have anything in common? What do you think Shakespeare intended by his presentation of these two characters?

# Good and evil

A leading theme in *Macbeth* is the battle between good and evil. Most critics agree that Shakespeare intended Macbeth to be seen initially as a good man, tempted into evil by the Witches and by his wife. He is almost always presented as such on stage.

Shakespeare uses the words 'good' and 'goodness' and 'bad', 'ill', 'evil', 'worse' and 'worst' throughout the play, inviting the reader to reflect upon ideas about good and evil that are so clearly portrayed through the action. The concepts of salvation and damnation are closely associated with the good/evil opposition and the words 'devil' and 'angel' appear in equal number in the play.

## Activity 3

Working in teams, see how quickly you can identify the characters who speak the following lines:

a) **'now I am bent to know,/ By the worst means, the worst;'**
(Act 3, Scene 4)

b) **'Things at the worst will cease, or else climb upward/ To what they were before.'** (Act 4, Scene 2)

c) **'Not in the legions/ Of horrid hell can come a devil more damn'd/ In evils to top Macbeth.'** (Act 4, Scene 3)

d) **'Now we'll together, and the chance of goodness/ Be like our warranted quarrel.'** (Act 4, Scene 3)

e) **'to do harm/ Is often laudable, to do good sometime/ Accounted dangerous folly.'** (Act 4, Scene 2)

f) **'Good things of day begin to droop and drowse,/ While night's black agents to their preys do rouse.'** (Act 3, Scene 2)

Macbeth begins the play winning honours for himself through his bravery in the service of his king. The supernaturally inspired prospect of the crown makes Macbeth susceptible to his wife's entreaties that he should murder Duncan, against his conscience, but immediately he has done the 'deed', he wishes it undone and is full of guilt.

We see how, having done one foul deed, Macbeth persuades himself that he must commit more murder to protect his position; evil multiplies and the good *within* Macbeth is conquered by evil. The next stage in the play shows how the good *outside* Macbeth conspires against him and brings about the victory of goodness over evil.

# Appearance and reality

At the heart of *Macbeth* lies the equivocation of the Witches. They speak the truth, but they conceal the truth too. They appear to be guiding Macbeth but in reality they are luring him to his doom and damnation.

> **Key quotations**
>
> 'Fair is foul, and foul is fair,' *(All Witches, Act 1, Scene 1)*

Lady Macbeth encourages Macbeth to assume a false face to conceal his true intentions towards Duncan, so that Duncan sees Macbeth as a **'peerless kinsman'** *(Act 1, Scene 4)* even while Macbeth is plotting to take his life.

In public, Macbeth appears to trust and value Banquo; he seems sincere when he calls Banquo **'our chief guest'** *(Act 3, Scene 1)*, urging him to **'Fail not our feast'** when he privately knows that he will be murdered before the banquet begins.

Lady Macbeth is also very skilled at appearing to be something she isn't. She warmly welcomes Duncan to her castle, although she knows he is to be murdered there. She also appears shocked at the news of his murder and she pretends to faint, despite having seen the dead king herself. She also disguises her true feelings at the banquet as she watches Macbeth lose control of himself.

Even the good character Malcolm pretends to be bad in order to test Macduff's integrity in Act 4, Scene 3.

When Macduff makes the shocking revelation that **'Macduff was from his mother's womb/ Untimely ripp'd'** *(Act 5, Scene 8)*, Macbeth finally grasps the reality of his situation.

> **Key quotations**
>
> **And be these juggling fiends no more believ'd**
> **That palter with us in a double sense,**
> **That keep the word of promise to our ear**
> **And break it to our hope.**
> *(Macbeth, Act 5, Scene 8)*

Shakespeare uses the words 'seem', 'face', 'false' and 'hide' to highlight the importance of appearance and reality throughout the play.

**Activity 4**

What other examples can you find of the difference between appearance and reality in the play?

# Scotland – the health of the nation

Shakespeare probably wrote *Macbeth* in honour of King James I, as the plot depicts the founding of his family dynasty, the Stuart kings.

### James I of England and VI of Scotland

James Stewart, son of Mary Queen of Scots, came to the throne of Scotland as James VI in 1567. He then also succeeded Elizabeth I in 1603, when she died without children, to become James I of England and Ireland. He reigned all three kingdoms for a further 22 years.

There are many references comparing the kingdom of Scotland with a sick or injured body in need of a cure. Words such as 'health', 'sickness', 'disease', 'fever', 'medicine' and 'purge' occur frequently, especially in the second half of the play when the forces of good are rallying to overthrow Macbeth.

### Key quotations

Let's make us med'cines of our great revenge
To cure this deadly grief.
*(Malcolm, Act 4, Scene 3)*

Meet we the med'cine of the sickly weal,
And with him pour we in our country's purge,
Each drop of us.
*(Caithness, Act 5, Scene 2)*

If thou couldst, doctor, cast
The water of my land, find her disease,
And purge it to a sound and pristine health,
I would applaud thee to the very echo
That should applaud again.
*(Macbeth, Act 5, Scene 3)*

When Macbeth refers to Scotland as an invalid, the audience realize he seems more concerned for his country than he appeared to be before and this is one of the ways that Shakespeare retains sympathy for him, despite his terrible deeds.

# Ambition and the supernatural

Other significant themes of ambition and the supernatural in *Macbeth* are sometimes linked. Both Macbeth and Lady Macbeth are ambitious for the crown. Whether Macbeth's ambition somehow invited the visitation of the Witches or whether the predictions of the Witches awakened unnatural ambition in him is a question for debate. Lady Macbeth's ambition was swiftly aroused by Macbeth's letter and she immediately called upon dark spirits to aid her in her murderous plot.

Are the Witches really supernatural beings, interfering old women or just figments of Macbeth's imagination?

# Other themes

Other significant themes in the play can be expressed as opposites, as with appearance and reality, because the play is really about a clash between what is right and what is wrong in human action and this lends itself to a series of **antithetical** ideas and images:

- life and death
- order and chaos
- sleep and restlessness.

**antithetical** directly opposed

## Writing about themes

*Upgrade*

In your assessment, you may be asked to write about an individual theme or pair of themes. There are different ways that such questions might be asked.

You might be asked how Shakespeare presents a theme, e.g. How does Shakespeare present the theme of ambition in Macbeth? This type of question requires that you think about the methods that the playwright has used to convey this theme.

You might be asked to consider the relative importance of a theme, for example:

- How important do you think the themes of good and evil are in the play?
- How far do you consider the play to be about kingship?

To answer this type of question, you should consider how the theme relates to Shakespeare's main purpose and message, and how it compares to other significant themes.

# The play in production

Plays are written to be performed either live on stage or filmed for a TV or cinema audience. Any such performance is called a production and is the result of collaboration between a director and a cast of actors, supported by a design team responsible for setting and **props**, costume, lighting and sound. This production team all work together on the playwright's **script** to find ways to bring the play to life for an audience.

> **props** moveable objects used on stage by the actors
>
> **script** the written version of a play as used in rehearsals for a performance

## The director

*Macbeth* is one of the most frequently staged of Shakespeare's plays and is hugely popular with audiences. Successive directors have interpreted the play through the ages, grappling with questions such as: How are the Witches to be presented? Is Macbeth's 'dagger of the mind' real or imaginary? Such questions have been especially pertinent in the 20th and 21st centuries, when modern theatre technology allowed the creation of all sorts of special effects on stage.

> ### Activity 1
>
> Make a list of the aspects of the play that you think are open to interpretation.

No two directors of *Macbeth* will ever make exactly the same decisions about how to present the various characters or which themes to emphasize. For example, it is possible to direct the actor playing Lady Macbeth to be hard and unfeeling, incapable of understanding her husband's conscience, dismissive of his scruples and scornful of his horrified reaction to having murdered Duncan. Or she could be directed to be very feminine in her attempt to persuade Macbeth to murder the king; she could weep when recalling her nursing baby, using physical closeness and tears to wheedle her husband into doing what she wants.

It is the director's job to study and re-read the play many times before making crucial decisions about what he or she wants the audience to take away from the performance. For example, should the audience be made to confront the consequences of ambition? Or is it more important for them to re-think their attitudes towards the supernatural or to contemplate the presence of evil in apparently normal people? Making decisions like these will help the director to create an individual interpretation of the play.

Other decisions that have to be made by a director relate to the acting and to the design of the play.

# The actors

Even before rehearsals begin, the director will have made decisions about casting the roles that will affect the way the audience responds to individual characters. The director will be looking for particular physical qualities in terms of age, build, colouring, facial features and vocal qualities, which best fit each character.

**Activity 2**

Imagine you are putting on a performance of Macbeth. Write down the physical and vocal qualities that you would want the actors of the following characters to possess:

- Macbeth
- Lady Macbeth
- Macduff
- Lady Macduff
- Hecate.

**a)** Think about what each actor's build and height should be, together with any further physical characteristics that you think are important.

**b)** Think about what his or her voice should be like (e.g. try to suggest a pitch, pace and accent for each character).

**c)** Give reasons for your choices based on your knowledge of the text.

The casting of Duncan is critical in how the audience react to his murder and therefore how they react to the whole play. Lady Macbeth refers to him as an old man but age is always relative. An audience will react differently to the murder of an athletic-looking 55 year old than they will to the murder of a frail 80 year old. In one recent production, directed by Declan Donnellan, Duncan was depicted as blind, increasing his vulnerability and utter dependence upon the protection of his hosts.

**Activity 3**

Working in a small group, act out Act 1, Scene 6, showing the arrival of Duncan and his interaction with his **'honour'd hostess'**. See how many different interpretations of the role of Duncan you can achieve.

Lady Macbeth welcomes King Duncan to the castle

One of the most important aspects of any Shakespeare play in performance is how clearly the language is delivered to make sense of Shakespeare's verse and densely packed imagery for the audience. This is also a challenge for the director, who works closely with the actors to hammer out the meaning of each line so that it can be delivered in such a way as to communicate with a 21st-century audience, who may find the language difficult.

## Activity 4

Compare the delivery of Macbeth's soliloquy from Act 2, Scene 1 – **'Is this a dagger which I see before me'** – as performed by at least two of the following actors.

- Ian McKellen (Royal Shakespeare Company (RSC), 1976) – available on DVD and extracts on the Internet

- Anthony Sher (Roundhouse, 2001) – available on DVD and extracts on the Internet

- Jon Finch (Polanski film, 1972) – available on DVD and extracts on the Internet

- Patrick Stewart (BBC, 2009) – available on DVD and extracts on the Internet

Actors do not merely speak their lines to bring the speeches to life; they must physically embody their roles and interact with their fellow actors in a believable way in order to make the action of the play appear real to the audience. This involves consistently reacting to the events of the play and the speeches of others, using both physical and facial expression. Of course, in *Macbeth*, many of the events are 'unnatural', 'supernatural' or, at the very least, unexpected, so the actors have often to find non-verbal ways to show extremes of feeling to the audience.

## Activity 5

Make suggestions about how an actor playing the part of Macbeth could use facial expressions and physical actions to show his reactions at the following key moments in the play:

- the first appearance of the Witches and their sudden disappearance (Act 1, Scene 3)
- Ross' announcement that Macbeth is now Thane of Cawdor (Act 1, Scene 3)
- the appearance of the dagger that leads Macbeth to Duncan (Act 2, Scene 1)
- the knocking at the gate (Act 2, Scene 2)
- the appearance of Banquo's ghost (Act 3, Scene 4)
- the show of apparitions (Act 4, Scene 1)
- the death of Lady Macbeth (Act 5, Scene 5)
- the news that Birnam Wood is moving (Act 5, Scene 5)
- Macduff's revelation that he was not **'of woman born'** (Act 5, Scene 8).

### Key fact

In Shakespeare's time, all the female roles were played by young men. There were no actresses on the English stage until 1660.

## Activity 6

Imagine you are directing the actors playing Macbeth and Lady Macbeth in Act 3, Scene 4.

a) Add a brief direction for each of the lines from **'It will have blood they say...'** to the end of the scene to guide the actor in how to deliver the lines.

b) Write a paragraph explaining how these directions support your interpretation of Macbeth, Lady Macbeth and their relationship at this point in the play.

## Stage setting

A stage designer will work closely with the director to achieve the setting that the director wants. Although the action of the play takes place in 11th-century Scotland, it is quite usual for contemporary productions to offer a timeless feel to the setting or update the action to modern times.

This Australian film of *Macbeth* had a modern-day gangster setting; all the actors spoke in Australian accents

While the play's requirements in terms of the settings are not complicated, the play's action suggests the following locations:

- a heath
- Duncan's headquarters
- Macbeth's castle at Dunsinane with both inner chambers and the castle approach
- a banqueting hall
- Macduff's castle in Fife
- the English court
- battlefields and exterior scenes in general.

It is possible to play the whole tragedy on an empty space with occasional pieces of set and props – chairs, tables, goblets and so forth – much as it was performed in Shakespeare's day.

It is unusual for modern productions to attempt **scenic realism** because of the swift-moving action of the play which, over 29 scenes, would be slowed down unacceptably by too many scene changes.

The 1976 Trevor Nunn production of the play, with Ian McKellan and Judi Dench in the lead roles, was set on a bare stage with the actors performing within a circle formed by wooden boxes that made up the only set. The play was performed as timeless, with the different settings created through the poetry of Shakespeare's language and the imagination of the audience.

Other modern directors and designers have chosen to **transpose** the play to a more specific modern era and to use adaptable or **composite settings**. For example, in the Patrick Stewart production of the play, directed by Rupert Goold (stage 2007, film

2009), the play is transposed to a **totalitarian state** based in war-torn Scotland in the mid-20<sup>th</sup> century.

In this version, designer Anthony Ward created a composite setting to resemble the white-tiled spaces of an underground hospital, kitchen, morgue or torture chamber. The setting was altered in appearance for different scenes using various metal trolleys and slabs; upstage were the metal grilles of a cranking lift, which was used for shock entrances of, for example, the truly scary Witches. A large white sink was used for rinsing blood-coated hands. Larger pieces of setting were trucked on for individual scenes such as the banquet scene.

Macbeth, as king, became a Stalin-like tyrant figure in regimental uniform, his blown-up photograph dominating the public spaces in the castle. The Witches were played as terrifying nurses in a military hospital, dressed in spruce nurses' uniforms that became blood-spattered as the play proceeded. Banquo was murdered in a rocking railway carriage. It was the work of a highly inventive, if unorthodox, designer.

Whatever style the director chooses for the production, it's important to accommodate the speed of the action and to reflect the dark nature of its themes.

> **composite setting** a setting that serves the whole play but can be adapted for individual scenes
>
> **scenic realism** an approach to set design that attempts to create an illusion of reality through detailed settings of interiors
>
> **totalitarian state** a country run by a dictator who allows no opposition
>
> **transpose** to move the setting and/or period of a play from its original setting or context to a suitable or parallel context

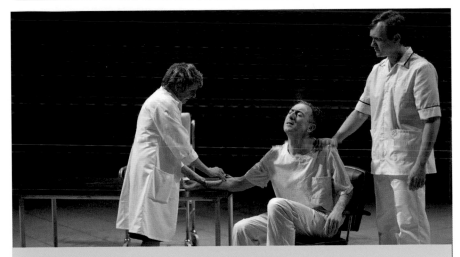

This production of *Macbeth* was set in a military hospital

> **Stalin**
>
> Joseph Stalin was the supreme ruler of the Soviet Union from the late 1920s until his death in 1953. He is considered to be one of the most ruthless of all political dictators of the 20th century and was responsible for the deaths of tens of millions of his own people.

**Activity 7**

Design a stage setting for a new production of *Macbeth*. Ask yourself how your ideas will help to convey Shakespeare's themes and intentions to an audience.

## Costume

Whether the director/designer has chosen to use a bare stage setting or an elaborate representation of solid rooms and outdoor spaces, the choice of costume is critical in conveying the chosen period setting to the audience.

Some designers opt for a sense of timelessness through their costume design, with the intention of suggesting that the issues of the play are relevant to all societies throughout the ages. Others, like Anthony Ward in the Rupert Goold production, aim to emphasize the similarities between the politics of Shakespeare's time, reflected in his depiction of 11th-century Scotland, and the politics of the 20th century.

Whatever period is chosen, the costume designer needs to convey the different ranks of the characters, be they king, prince, thane, captain or soldier. This can be done very simply or in great detail. We need to see the change in status of Macbeth and Lady Macbeth from thane and lady to king and queen, and this can also be achieved through costume.

For example, in Trevor Nunn's production the costumes were remarkably plain. All the company wore dark-coloured basic costumes, reflecting the darkness of the play, apart from Duncan, who was played by the elderly, white-haired and white-bearded Griffith Jones, dressed from head to toe in white, ceremonial robes, creating the impression of a child's view of God himself. Macbeth's rise to power was shown in an inserted coronation scene, where he wore a sumptuously ornamented robe, while Lady Macbeth had a simple gold coronet placed over the black turban that she wore throughout the play.

In other productions, notably Polanski's film version with Jon Finch and Francesca Annis (1972) and the 1997 film starring Jason Connery and Helen Baxendale, costumes appear approximately authentic to the 11th century; the men wear kilt-like skirts and there is no attempt to take the play out of its time. Controversially, at the time, in Polanski's film, Lady Macbeth performed the sleepwalking scene in the nude.

**Tips for assessment**

If you get the chance to see this play on stage, pay special attention to the way costume is used to signify period and/or create political parallels. Discuss and make notes about this aspect of the performance afterwards. You may refer to these details in your assessment where it is relevant to the question.

## Lighting and sound design

Originally the play would have been performed in daylight, with props of candles, flaming torches and lanterns used to suggest the very many night-time settings of the play. Modern productions have all the new technologies of the 21ˢᵗ century at their disposal and yet *Macbeth* is a play that is often performed under the simplest of lighting designs.

Because of its predominantly dark atmosphere, it is fairly traditional for the play to be performed without bright lights and sometimes scenes are set in semi-darkness. A recent exception was the Rupert Goold production, which was brightly lit for the most part with a harsh and cold white light; at other times the walls were bathed in a blood-red colour; pulsating light was also used to create an electrical otherworldliness for the weird sisters.

## The play in performance

When studying *Macbeth*, it is really useful to see a live production in the theatre. There are also several really good film versions of the play, a number of which are filmed versions of original theatre productions.

## Differences between theatre and film

There are a number of crucial differences between film and theatre in terms of what a theatre director and a film director can potentially achieve.

| | Plays performed on stage | Film versions of plays |
| --- | --- | --- |
| Setting | The action of the play must be depicted in a single stage space although the space may be transformed into a series of different settings, using stage mechanics to create the illusion of different locations. | The action of the play may be depicted as occurring in any number of different locations – both interior and exterior – and in any part of the world. These settings will appear to be real. |
| Time | A stage play follows the chronology (time sequence) as written by the playwright. | A film may include flashbacks and flash forwards. |
| The text | Most plays are produced in their entirety with few cuts made to the original text. | Directors often cut sections of text, preferring to replace them with film images of what is being said or described. |
| Action | References to events that occur offstage are used to give the audience necessary information to help them to understand the story. | 'Offstage' action may be portrayed in the film, becoming a fully realized part of the story. |
| Characters | Characters that do not appear on stage are referred to or described by the onstage actors. | The director may choose to use actors to portray these characters in the film; then descriptions of them can be dispensed with. |
| Audience view | From their seats in the auditorium, the audience, who can see the whole stage, choose who and/or what to watch. | The director chooses every shot of the film; the audience must watch the character selected by the director, so their experience is more closely shaped by the director. |
| Actors | The audience can be some distance away, so the actors must project their voices and ensure that their gestures and facial expressions are clearly defined. The audience listen to the dialogue to make sense of the play and understand each character's feelings. | A film actor can be more subtle; the director can choose close-ups to highlight significant moments and facial expressions. The director occasionally chooses to use a voice-over to explain the feelings of a particular character. |
| Performance | As the actors and action is live, no two performances (even by the same cast) are ever identical. | The film performance is captured for ever; it never changes. |

# Film versions of the play

Roman Polanski's 1972 film version, with a screenplay by Polanski and Kenneth Tynan, is viewed by many as the classic film adaptation of the play, but the original text is quite heavily cut. Polanski makes some bold interpretative decisions. The Witches open the film on a wide expanse of beach where they bury a severed hand with a dagger in its grasp. One Witch is blind, one very old and one is a young woman.

Polanski's film could set scenes in real-life landscapes that are not possible on stage

Macbeth and Lady Macbeth are portrayed as quite young and Polanski also includes a scene to show the murder of Duncan. When Macbeth returns to speak to the 'weird sisters', he discovers a coven of witches of all ages, shapes and sizes engaged in some kind of naked ritual. As a twist at the end of the film, we see Donaldbain seeking out the Witches. Some interpret this as Polanski suggesting that the cycle of evil is not over and that Malcolm's crown may also be under threat from a jealous brother.

Another film adaptation of *Macbeth* is the 1997 film version directed by Jeremy Freeston and starring Jason Connery and Helen Baxendale. This is a very accessible version although there are some cuts, principally from Act 5. Authentic period costume and sweeping shots of the rugged Scottish landscape give this film a truly historical feel.

The Japanese film *Throne of Blood* was closely based on *Macbeth*. Made in 1957 by legendary filmmaker Akira Kurosawa, this film fuses Shakespeare's plot with formal elements of Japanese theatre to make a very powerful adaptation of the play set in feudal Japan. Filmed in black and white, this is a mesmerizing version, memorable for its depiction of the haunted forest swathed in mists and for Macbeth's final moments as he is killed with a flight of hundreds of arrows.

# Filmed theatre productions

Trevor Nunn's 1976 production of the play, starring Ian McKellan and Judi Dench, was filmed in 1979 and presented a slightly reworked version of their original stage play. This is a very powerful straightforward production of the play with a stellar cast headed by two classically trained actors at the peak of their professional careers. Duncan is given almost holy status in this production through his frail appearance, white garments and constant acts of prayer, making his murder seem more monstrous to the audience.

Another filmed RSC production was directed by Greg Doran in 1999, with Anthony Sher and Harriet Walters in the lead roles. Doran's interpretation suggests parallels between the situation in Macbeth's Scotland and the civil war in Bosnia. It is a modern-dress production performed with minimal set. Macbeth is the returning war hero in military dress. In addition to their scripted performances, the Witches appear from under the banqueting table in Act 3 having produced the shocking apparition of Banquo, rocking the table and smashing the crockery so violently that Lady Macbeth's line about **'admir'd disorder'** *(Act 3, Scene 4)* is made to appear literal. Lady Macduff is murdered against a backdrop of drying washing with blankets, sheets and baby clothes becoming stained with blood.

The 2009 film version of Rupert Goold's production, starring Patrick Stewart and Kate Fleetwood, has already been mentioned on page 56. This is one of the most thrilling versions of the play. Macbeth is played as a man of late middle age who lives in a brutal world and becomes even more brutalized in the course of the play. The apparition scene is especially macabre as the Witches appear to revive corpses in a mortuary to speak the predictions to **'beware Macduff'** *(Act 4, Scene 1)* and others.

## Activity 8

Watch excerpts of one of the above productions on DVD or the Internet. Write a review saying why you think the interpretation of the play is valid or not.

# *Macbeth* on the Jacobean stage

When *Macbeth* was first staged, the King's Men did not have quite as many choices to make as a 21st-century theatre company. In public performances (as opposed to private performances before the king and his court), the play would have been performed either outdoors at the Globe Theatre in the afternoon or at an indoor theatre, like the Blackfriars Theatre, in the evening.

The stage at the Globe Theatre was a large raised rectangular space that jutted out into the audience at the front. At the rear of the stage space, there were two doors for entrances and exits. There were trapdoors in the stage, which were used for the entrance of supernatural figures; for example, the Witches might have appeared and disappeared from trapdoors to surprise Macbeth and Banquo in Act 1. There was also a balcony above the stage at the back where actors could appear.

In terms of acting, there is no one consensus about the delivery style of the actors' performances. On the one hand, the sheer size of the audience and the likelihood of constant background noise support the theory that Shakespearean actors had to declaim their words loudly and clearly, projecting their voices out to the audience. On the other hand, there are also lines and moments in *Macbeth* that suggest quite naturalistic performances. For example, in Act 5, Scene 1, the Doctor describes a series of detailed actions that Lady Macbeth performs as she sleepwalks; **'Look how she rubs her hands'** and Malcolm tells Macduff, at the end of Act 4, Scene 3, **'What, man, ne'er pull your hat upon your brows:/ Give sorrow words;'**. These examples suggest far more subtlety from the actors than simply reciting the lines.

## Writing about performance

*Upgrade*

When you are writing about *Macbeth* in your assessment, remember to write about Shakespeare's intentions for the audience rather than the reader, as it is the audience that the playwright is addressing. Even if you do not have an opportunity to see the play at the theatre, you need to think about the effects that are created for the audience as the action unfolds on stage, and reflect this in your answers.

Remember, however, that you must write about the text as Shakespeare wrote it and do not be tempted to make references to film versions unless you are writing a formal comparison between the two versions or making a point that is precisely relevant to the question asked.

## Skills for the assessment

Make sure you are fully prepared for the challenges of the assessment by following these practical steps.

### Step 1: Make sure you know the play really well

*Macbeth* is quite a short play, although it is a challenging play to understand, so you should try to read it at least four times before your assessment and watch as many live or filmed versions as you can.

As you re-read the play, make notes under the following headings:

- plot and structure
- context
- characters
- language
- themes
- performance.

### Step 2: Revision

Go back through this book and check that you have completed all of the activities. Re-read the key quotations from the play that appear throughout this book and try to learn as many as you can.

#### Extracts

Plan potential questions. For example, open the play randomly at any page and write at least one paragraph about the significance of the section in relation to the list of bullet points in Step 1.

#### Characters

Choose one of the characters from the play to focus on. Practise writing a page or more about how Shakespeare presents the character and his or her function in the play. Repeat the task for other characters.

#### Themes

Choose one of the following themes and practise writing a page or more about its importance in the play: kingship; appearance and reality; manhood; equivocation/ deceit; order and disorder; ambition; the influence of the supernatural.

Repeat the task for other themes.

**Activity 1**

Look back at the pages you have written about themes and characters. Find relevant quotations from the play that will help to support your ideas.

## Step 3: Improving exam technique

If you are sitting an exam on your set text, brushing up on exam technique is really worth the effort and can make a real difference to your overall grade. Below are some examples of question types that may come up in your exam.

### Essay-style questions

Most essay-style questions ask you to write about the plot (the events that take place in the play), structure (how events are organized), characters or themes. Here are some typical essay-style questions, with key words and phrases underlined. This is followed by an explanation of what each question requires.

> How does Shakespeare present Lady Macbeth in Act 1 of the play?

This question is about character and the 'how' part of the question refers to Shakespeare's methods. The writer's methods for creating character include:

- what the character looks/sounds like
- what the character says about himself/herself and about others
- what other characters say about the character
- how the character might be compared/contrasted with others
- what the character does – his/her actions and/or reactions in the play
- what kind of language the character uses when speaking.

> How is the theme of ambition presented in *Macbeth*?

This question is about theme and the 'how' part of the question refers to the methods that the playwright has used to convey this theme.

> *Macbeth* is sometimes described as a play of striking contrasts. Do you agree with this description?

This question is about the nature of the play as a whole. 'Do you agree?' means that you should weigh up the evidence for agreeing with the description and provide evidence to support your views. A good way to approach this type of question is to consider the appropriateness of the statement in relation to plot, structure, characters, themes, mood/atmosphere and language.

## Activity 2

Create a plan for the example question above, including details and quotations from the text. Try to organize your plan so that related points are grouped together. Possible points to consider include:

- contrasts between the reign of King Duncan and the reign of Macbeth
- Macbeth's and Banquo's contrasting reactions to the Witches' prophecies
- contrasts between the characters of Lady Macbeth and Lady Macduff
- contrasting themes in the play, such as order and disorder, appearance and reality, the natural and supernatural worlds, loyalty and treachery
- contrasting motifs such as sickness and health, sleep and sleeplessness, manliness and beastliness, truth and lies, darkness and light
- the way the play shifts between scenes of good and evil
- contrasts in mood and atmosphere.

### Extract-based questions

For extract-based questions you should look at past paper questions to familiarize yourself with the type of question that is specific to the exam you are going to take. You will have to practise reading the printed extract carefully and working with language on a detailed level.

When writing answers to extract-based questions, use a pen or highlighter to underline key words or phrases in the extract that strike you as important. It can be helpful to write very brief notes in the margin to remind you why you decided to pick out the phrases.

## Step 4: Answering the question

Always try to think ahead before you start writing. Thinking and planning ahead will help you to:

- structure your answer logically
- target the precise demands of the question
- avoid missing out points that are crucial to your argument
- include appropriate quotations.

Plans can take a variety of forms. However, a brief list is often the most helpful as it allows you to put your ideas into a logical sequence. In an exam, you should plan quickly. Don't spend more than about six or seven minutes on a plan. Jot down your ideas and away you go!

Develop your answer, step by step, building your argument by referring to precise moments from the play. Always support your ideas with short, relevant quotations from the play.

The best way to use a quotation is to absorb it into your own sentences. For example:

> Macbeth's decision to 'proceed no further' with the 'business' of killing Duncan is met with a barrage of protests from Lady Macbeth who succeeds in convincing him that going back on 'this enterprise' and betraying her hopes is worse than killing a king.

# Sample questions

**1**

Answer parts a) and b).

**a)** How does Shakespeare present Lady Macbeth's attitudes towards Macbeth in this extract from Act 1, Scene 5?

| | |
|---|---|
| **Macbeth** | My dearest love, |
| | Duncan comes here tonight. |
| **Lady Macbeth** | And when goes hence? |
| **Macbeth** | Tomorrow, as he purposes. |
| **Lady Macbeth** | O never |
| | Shall sun that morrow see. |
| | Your face, my thane, is as a book where men |
| | May read strange matters. To beguile the time, |
| | Look like the time, bear welcome in your eye, |
| | Your hand, your tongue; look like th'innocent flower, |
| | But be the serpent under't. He that's coming |
| | Must be provided for, and you shall put |
| | This night's great business into my dispatch, |
| | Which shall to all our nights and days to come |
| | Give solely sovereign sway and masterdom. |
| **Macbeth** | We will speak further – |
| **Lady Macbeth** | Only look up clear; |
| | To alter favour ever is to fear. |
| | Leave all the rest to me. |

**b)** How does Shakespeare present Lady Macbeth's attitudes towards Macbeth in a **different** part of the play?

**83**

**2**

How does Shakespeare present Macbeth so that, despite his terrible actions, the audience never completely loses sympathy for him?

**3**

Choose two scenes from *Macbeth* where Shakespeare creates high tension for his audience and explain the methods that he uses to achieve this tension.

**4**

How does Shakespeare explore the themes of appearance and reality in *Macbeth*?

**5**

Remind yourself of Act 1, Scene 5 and its importance within the play. Starting with this scene, explore the ways in which Lady Macbeth is presented in the text and in one or more performed versions of the play (e.g. audio, television, graphic novel or film).

**6**

Choose a key theme from *Macbeth*. Compare your reading of the theme in the play with the way the same theme is treated in an adaptation of the play (e.g. audio, television, graphic novel or film).
In your comparison you should:
- show your understanding of the whole play
- explain your understanding of the differences between the presentation of the theme in the original play and its presentation in your chosen adaptation
- explore the reasons why the adaptation is different from the original play.
Refer to both the play text and the adaptation to support your answer.

# Sample answers

## Sample answer 1

Below is a sample answer from a student, together with examiner comments, to the following question on the play:

> The 'good' characters in the play are all fairly uninspiring. Do you agree?

Shows a clear focus on the question.

Reference to differences between the good characters is useful, but 'Take Duncan' is overly casual for a written assessment.

This needs to be put into context. When does Duncan do this? A quotation would be useful.

This assertion needs to be linked to the question or to a quotation.

Reference to the act/scene would be helpful.

This is a good return to the 'uninspiring' idea and gives some insight into the contrast between Duncan's trusting nature and Macbeth's suspicion.

This is another casual phrase that is not a complete sentence.

Shows very good use of quotation.

Good understanding is shown here.

This assertion needs support.

I don't agree that the good characters in the play are uninspiring. They are each very different in the way they respond to evil. Take Duncan. He is an old and wise king who cares for his country and his thanes. He seems almost unaware of evil around him. He is grateful to Macbeth and Banquo for saving Scotland from the rebels and he rewards Macbeth and promises to reward Banquo. It doesn't seem to cross his mind that anyone would want to kill him and when he announces that Malcolm will be the next king, he doesn't seem to realize that he is also endangering his son's life. Maybe he is too good for his own good.

He calls Macbeth 'worthiest cousin' and later sends a diamond to Lady Macbeth only minutes before the couple murder him. I think Shakespeare wanted the audience to see a good man but one who needed a bit more understanding of the messy world of politics. Still, it is not uninspiring to see a good and trusting man who everyone seems to think was a really good king, even if being so trusting costs him his life. Macbeth is not a trusting king at all but that did not save him either.

Then there's Banquo. He is a good friend to Macbeth. But unlike Duncan, he can see the bad around him. He warns Macbeth not to trust the Witches who he sees as 'instruments of darkness' who might betray Macbeth 'in deepest consequence', and they do.

Although Banquo does not act upon the Witches' predictions, he is troubled by the meeting with them and avoids sleep because he fears the dreams and 'cursed thoughts' that have disturbed his rest since the meeting. He confides in Macbeth that he has dreamed of the Witches, saying 'to you they have shown some truth', but Macbeth is too busy thinking about killing Duncan to talk to Banquo and puts off any discussion to another time.

He does test Banquo, though, suggesting that if Banquo will follow him – 'cleave to my consent' – in the future, 'It shall make honour for you'. This is where Banquo makes his big mistake, because he thinks Macbeth is suggesting something that is not honourable. He tells Macbeth that he will be guided by him but only if he can keep his 'allegiance clear' meaning loyalty to King Duncan. I think this is brave of Banquo, not 'uninspiring' like the question says. It inspires me to see that Banquo is honourable and will not be corrupted by Macbeth. Unfortunately, being honourable got him murdered.

*Shows good understanding.*

*The 'big mistake' is a little colloquial.*

*This is a good reference to the terms of the question.*

Banquo and Macduff both seem a bit suspicious of Macbeth after Duncan's body is found. Macduff questions Macbeth over his killing of the grooms, asking him 'Wherefore did you so?', thinking Macbeth had killed possible witnesses to the murder. Macbeth remembers this later and decides to kill Macduff's family to get back at him for not trusting him and not going to his coronation.

*This isn't quite accurate; it is Macduff's fleeing to England that seals the fate of his family.*

Banquo is also suspicious, because he is the one who knows what the Witches predicted for Macbeth and maybe put two and two together after meeting Macbeth late at night when Macbeth was going to Duncan's chamber to kill him; also he had his dagger with him. So he makes it clear again that he is honourable saying he is against 'treasonous malice' and swearing this by 'the great hand of God'. Macbeth picks up on this too and decides that he will kill his friend because he is both brave and wise, and therefore a threat to him when he is king.

*Although this may be so, Shakespeare does not tell us that this is what made Banquo suspicious.*

Another way that Banquo's goodness is not uninspiring is when he promises not to miss the feast, saying 'My lord, I will not.' Then, even after Macbeth has him murdered, he shows up at the feast after all and scares Macbeth witless.

*Although focused on the question, the 'scared witless' phrase is too colloquial for written assessment.*

This candidate reveals a secure grasp of the play and there is some insight here. The question of good characters being 'uninspiring' is addressed directly and the focus is maintained. However, the ideas need to be better structured and there are occasional lapses in expression in an answer that shows good knowledge and understanding.

# Sample answer 2

Below is a sample answer from a student, together with examiner comments, to the following question on the play:

> How important is the theme of deception in *Macbeth*?

This is a very clear introduction, focused and crisp.

I believe that deception is the most important theme in 'Macbeth'. The Witches deceive Macbeth when they first accost him on the heath and they deceive him again when he visits them in Act 4, so that he believes he lives 'a charmed life' and cannot be defeated. In turn, Macbeth deceives Duncan about his true intentions and then, after the murder, he deceives the whole of Scotland as he shifts the blame for Duncan's death onto the innocent sons and claims the throne for himself. The whole action of the play, therefore, is based on deception.

This has the makings of an organized approach.

Shakespeare's characterization also supports the theme of deception. In Act 1, Scene 2, Duncan admits that he has been too trusting of the traitorous Thane of Cawdor and proclaims that he, 'No more... shall deceive our bosom interest' before, ironically, passing the thaneship on to 'noble Macbeth'.

The sensitivity to irony is good.

Shakespeare underlines the irony for us as Macbeth enters in Act 1, Scene 4, just as Duncan has commented on the impossibility of finding 'the mind's construction in the face' and is greeted with the warm welcome of 'Worthiest cousin'.

These are well-integrated quotations.

Duncan is deceived in his 'cousin', who within moments is contemplating leaping over all that stands in his way to achieve his 'black and deep desires'. And even before Macbeth is urged by his wife to 'look like the innocent flower/ But be the serpent under't' in the following scene, Macbeth is prepared to use deception as he speaks aside to himself in this scene, 'The eye wink at the hand', implying double dealing to come.

Focus is maintained and there is careful attention to Shakespeare's language.

However, it is probably Lady Macbeth, rather than her husband, that we think of when considering the importance of the theme of deception in the play. She greets the prospect of Macbeth becoming king and of becoming the queen herself with joy, but the language that she uses to Macbeth when he returns from the wars is full of references to deceit. She tells him to 'beguile the time' and to 'look up clear', disguising their murderous intentions.

In Scene 6, Lady Macbeth alone welcomes the king with 'false face' to the Castle that will 'host' Duncan's murder; she is obsequious towards the king and promises to 'rest your hermits', meaning that she and Macbeth will pray continuously for the good of the king. She is deception personified here.

Sensitive handling of language here, revealing secure understanding.

Nor does Lady Macbeth's ability to deceive end with her false words. It is she who decides to shift suspicion about the murder onto Duncan's grooms by smearing them with Duncan's blood; it is she who calmly considers a 'little water' capable of clearing the pair of the 'deed' of killing a king; and she that ensures that Macbeth appears in his nightgown 'lest occasion call us/And show us to be watchers'. When Macbeth reveals in Act 2, Scene 3 that he has killed the grooms in his 'fury', Lady Macbeth distracts attention away from him with a deceptive faint.

This draws a good distinction between what Lady Macbeth says to deceive and what she does.

The theme of deception is also linked to the notion of equivocation and here we find the Witches ability to 'palter' with Macbeth 'in a double sense' is crucial to the play's action and meaning. From the beginning of the play, their words have haunted Macbeth and although he has seen all three of their pronouncements about him come to fruition, he deceives himself into thinking that he can thwart their predictions about Banquo.

Good insight revealed here.

In Act 4, Scene 1, Macbeth visits the Witches for a second time. Now king, he is more insistent with the Witches, charging them to tell him the truth, '… shall Banquo's issue ever/Reign in this kingdom?' The Witches try to evade the question, in order to maintain their deception of him, instructing him, 'Seek to know no more'; but he is adamant, 'Let me know.' Macbeth's insistence on 'knowledge' and truth is ironic as he is living a lie; he pleads with the Witches, as Banquo's Ghost 'smiles upon' him, 'Is this so?' but in spite of their assurance 'all this is so', he clings to the implications that they have given him of his inability to be defeated.

This is another good paragraph, developing the argument about the importance of deception.

This is a fluently written response that is very well organized. In this extract, from the first half of the answer, we can see a methodical approach to the task. The candidate looks at the importance of deception to the action and plot of the play, at its importance in terms of character and then the theme of equivocation is linked purposefully to deception.

# Sample answer 3

Below is a sample answer from a student, together with examiner comments, to the following question on the play:

> Remind yourself of the opening scene of the play and its importance within *Macbeth*. Starting with this scene, explore the ways in which the Witches are presented in the text and in one or more performed versions of the play (e.g. audio, television, graphic novel or film).

Shows focus on the Witches.

This does not start with the opening scene. Macbeth does not call the Witches 'hags' until Act 4.

The Witches are very important in the play. They trick Macbeth. When he first meets them he is not scared of them. Macbeth is quite rude and calls them hags, but they don't seem to care. Banquo also says a rude thing to them and points at their beards.

This is about Macbeth's reactions, not about the way the Witches are presented.

When the Witches tell Macbeth that he will be king, he is shocked as the king is alive but after they have disappeared he is pleased to think he will be king.

This reference echoes the gist of Macbeth's speech in Act 4, but it needs to highlight how the Witches are presented.

Later in the play, Macbeth goes to find the Witches again and he does find them, but we don't know how he knew where to find them. They are not as friendly to Macbeth the second time and he is very angry with them. He says even if the whole world was to come crashing down they must tell him what he wants to know.

When Macbeth sees all the apparitions, they are mostly children. One is a bloody child and one is another child with a crown and a branch, and then there are more kings who all look like Banquo. Then Macbeth feels that he has done all his murders for Banquo's children and he is angry and damns all those that trust the Witches. This means he damns himself because even now he still trusts them that no man born of woman will harm him and that he will not be killed until the wood moves.

There is some understanding here of Macbeth's predicament and motivation.

In the film version I have seen by Roman Polanski, the Witches are the first thing you see on the screen. At first you can hardly see them because the camera is a long way away and then you see three black spots crawl into shot. The sequence takes a long time to play. As you get nearer to the Witches, one is very old and wrinkled and one is blind and very ugly and one is young with blond hair but not pretty. They are dragging something over the sand and then they start to dig a hole and they put a noose in

Describes the opening sequence of the Polanski film quite well.

it and a severed arm with a dagger. There is a lot of blood, which seeps into the sand.

This is not the same as Shakespeare's first scene where they are only on stage for about two minutes and they just plan to meet with Macbeth after the battle. In the play they all say 'Fair is foul, and foul is fair' and this matters because that is what the play shows us. You don't really know what is good or bad in this play as Macbeth starts off good but ends up very bad.

*An attempt to compare the two opening scenes; some understanding of language is shown.*

In the film, one of the Witches does a flash at Macbeth after they have hailed him and she runs away into the mist. When he goes back to see them in the film they are all naked and having an orgy and Macbeth is given a psychedelic drug to take and that's how he sees the apparitions; he is a bit sick like after you have had too much to drink and seems to go home on his own like after a party. But in the play he is angry and curses the Witches.

*This reference to another witch scene in the Polanski film lacks detail.*

In the film, Macbeth decides to kill Macduff's family after he has seen the Witches because of the drug that he drank, but in the play it is because Lennox tells him that Macduff has fled to England. We do not see the Witches again.

*This brief attempt to compare the play and the film is not very purposeful.*

This is quite a confused response that fails to find the correct focus as defined in the question. At times, expression is not entirely secure. There is some knowledge and understanding of the play and of Macbeth's attitudes, but there is an almost random feel to the contents of the answer. It is limited on language and 'importance'.

## Sample answer 4

Below is a sample answer from a student, together with examiner comments, to the following question on the play:

---

Answer parts a) and b).

**a)** How does Shakespeare present Macbeth's thoughts and feelings in this part of the play?

**Macbeth:**

We have scorch'd the snake, not kill'd it;
She'll close, and be herself, whilst our poor malice
Remains in danger of her former tooth.
But let the frame of things disjoint, both the worlds suffer,
Ere we will eat our meal in fear, and sleep
In the affliction of these terrible dreams
That shake us nightly, Better be with the dead
Whom we, to gain our peace, have sent to peace,
Than on the torture of the mind to lie
In restless ecstasy. Duncan is in his grave.
After life's fitful fever, he sleeps well;
Treason has done his worst; nor steel nor poison,
Malice domestic, foreign levy, nothing
Can touch him further.

*(Act 3, Scene 2)*

**b)** How does Shakespeare present Macbeth's thoughts and feelings in a different part of the play?

---

This is a very clear start, sensitive to the tone of the speech.

This extract is taken from Act 3 of the play; Macbeth has gained the crown by murdering Duncan and yet he is not contented. Shakespeare presents Macbeth in reflective but depressive mood, comparing his own anxiety and 'terrible dreams' with the peace that Duncan enjoys 'in his grave'. Not for the first time, Shakespeare shows Macbeth valuing sleep and peace from the perspective of a man suffering nightmares 'That shake us nightly'. Having 'murdered sleep' in Act 2, when he murdered Duncan, he now sees 'good repose' as an unattainable ideal.

A difficult image is unravelled and linked to Macbeth's state of mind.

Shakespeare has Macbeth begin his speech with one of many references in the play to the natural world. Here he imagines his enemy – Duncan and his sons, Malcolm and Donaldbain – to be like a snake that he has attacked and wounded but not killed.

He imagines the two sons coming together, perhaps like the forked tongue of a snake ready to attack him and topple him from the throne that he has gained through treachery. They will withstand the wound that he has delivered and recover. This is clearly a disturbing thought to Macbeth.

Shakespeare then shows us Macbeth's reckless attitude towards Scotland, and indeed to the universe as a whole, when he suggests that, as far as he is concerned, the 'frame of things' can be wrenched out of shape and both the world and the afterlife 'suffer' rather than he should endure more fear of discovery and of his enemies. He is determined to do something about it rather than 'eat our meal in fear' and is willing to sacrifice both this world and the next in attaining a sense of safety. This shows his insecure state of mind.

*This is good on Macbeth's feelings.*

In 'Macbeth', Shakespeare refers a number of times to eating/drinking/feasting and both the food imagery and the sleep imagery that is used in the play are associated with nourishment – both literal and spiritual. Here Macbeth pictures a simple meal and a sleep as enviable things to have – things he once took for granted before he murdered Duncan.

*Makes good link to the wider play.*

Shakespeare vividly conjures up Macbeth's guilt and regret when he compares himself unfavourably to dead Duncan; he envies him his peace. He sees a king now removed from the threat of treason, the worries of kingship and the threat of 'steel or poison'.

*Macbeth's guilt is noted clearly here.*

Macbeth uses the iambic pentameter, which he uses throughout the play, but there is a morose tone to this speech and a downward inflection to lines like 'Better be with the dead' and 'nothing/Can touch him further'. Shakespeare depicts Macbeth's disturbed state of mind through the use of hypersyllabic lines that disrupt the metre. This is especially effective at 'both the worlds suffer' which throws emphasis on the phrase and shows Macbeth's preoccupation with the afterlife and with his 'eternal jewel' – his soul – which he accepts he has sacrificed; and all to make the sons of Banquo king.

*Makes a brief but useful reference to metre.*

As in other parts of the play, Macbeth's speech has a number of contrasting words and ideas. The antithesis between good and bad is presented here in the word 'better' and the audience would be shocked at the negative thought. How can it ever be 'better' to be with the dead? On the other hand, Macbeth can see Duncan's current state as 'good' because he 'sleeps well'; again this is

*Demonstrates excellent close reading here.*

puzzling as we don't usually associate being dead with anything positive. The word 'bad' is also present in 'our poor malice' and 'malice domestic' (mal = bad) where Macbeth contemplates bad deeds close to home; and the superlative of 'bad' – 'worst' appears, too – 'treason has done his worst'. Through these antitheses, Shakespeare suggests Macbeth's feelings are in turmoil and it also reflects one of the central contrasts of the play – 'foul and fair'.

Overall, the language of the speech is violent – 'scorch'd', 'kill'd', 'affliction', 'shake', 'torture', 'steel', 'poison'. In this way Shakespeare presents Macbeth's thoughts and feelings to be violent, entirely apt for the once moral man now on the brink of committing the widespread bloodshed that will be a hallmark of his kingship.

This sensitive conclusion reveals knowledge of the whole play.

This is a sophisticated answer that reveals a secure understanding of the play and of Shakespeare's use of language and imagery within it. The candidate offers a very close and sensitive reading of the speech and ties thoughtful analysis to the question focus on thoughts and feelings in a purposeful way. The analysis of Shakespeare's manipulation of iambic pentameter to reflect the inner workings of Macbeth's mind is also creditworthy. This is very impressive work at this level.

# Glossary

**ambiguous** something that can be interpreted in different ways

**antithetical** directly opposed

**artefact** object or thing of cultural or historical interest

**blank verse** poetry that does not rhyme

**catalyst** an agent of change

**catastrophe** in Greek tragedy, the concluding part of the play where the protagonist accepts ruin

**catharsis** in Greek tragedy, an outrush of audience emotion; pity for the ruined hero and fear for their own fate

**climax** the highest or most intense part of the play or a turning-point in the action

**composite setting** a setting that serves the whole play but can be adapted for individual scenes

**couplet** two lines of verse, usually rhyming

**damnation** the belief in Christian teaching that the souls of sinners and criminals will be damned after death and burn in hell for eternity

**declaim** to pronounce words loudly and clearly in a precisely articulated manner

**discovery scene** where characters are discovered to surprise or shock the audience

**equivocation** the use of misleading, contradictory or ambiguous language intended to deceive others. The word is used a number of times in the play, especially in relation to the way the Witches deceive Macbeth into thinking he is invincible

**exposition** key information to help the audience make sense of the action and characters in the play

**figurative language** language that uses figures of speech, is metaphorical and not literal

**foil** a character whose function is to serve as a contrast to another character

**fulsome** flattering or gushing

**futility** pointlessness

**harangue** an angry, critical attack on someone

**iambic pentameter** a line of verse with ten syllables, where the stress falls on the second syllable (and then every other syllable) in the line, e.g. 'di dum' as in 'Throw <u>physic</u> to the <u>dogs</u>, I'll <u>none</u> of <u>it</u>' *(Act 5, Scene 3)*

**imagery** visually descriptive or figurative language

**irony** a literary technique where the intended meaning differs from what is said or presented directly

**issue** the collective term for children or descendants

**manifestation** the appearance of a ghost, spirit or supernatural event

**metaphor** the use of a word or phrase in a way that is not literal, e.g. Duncan's planting/ nurturing metaphor: 'I have begun to plant thee and will labour/ to make thee full of growing.' *(Act 1, Scene 4)*

**metre** the rhythm of lines of verse, dependent on the number of syllables in a line and the stress pattern

**motif** a word, phrase or image in literature that is repeated to create specific effects

**nemesis** in Greek tragedy, a person or force that inflicts punishment or revenge

**ominous** a warning sign

**paradoxical** contradictory or inconsistent ideas that are spoken as facts

**plagiarism** the illegal copying of someone else's work; a form of literary theft

**poetry** a relatively short piece of literature where meaning is conveyed through imagery and expressed using a set rhythm or rhyme

**proleptic irony** irony that occurs when a character says something that turns out to be more significant than appears at the time

**props** moveable objects used on stage by the actors

**prose** any writing in continuous form without rhythm or rhyme

**protagonist** the main character

**regicide** a king-killer

**remorse** a feeling of regret and repentance for having done something wrong

**Renaissance** the revival of classical styles of art and literature in Europe in the 14th–16th centuries

**reversal** *(peripeteia)* a reversal of fortunes

**rhyme** a similar sound in the ending of words, e.g. trouble/bubble

**rhyming couplet** when only two lines of poetry end in rhyme

**salvation** the belief in Christian teaching that good souls will go to heaven to be saved and live with God for ever

**scenic realism** an approach to set design that attempts to create an illusion of reality through detailed settings of interiors

**script** the written version of a play as used in rehearsals for a performance

**simile** a comparison of one thing with another, using 'as' or 'like', e.g. 'signs of nobleness like stars shall shine' *(Act 1, Scene 4)*

**soliloquy** where a character voices aloud their innermost thoughts for the audience to hear

**stichomythia** the rapid exchange of brief lines of dialogue

**thane** a title given in medieval times to the Scottish equivalent of an English Baron. The title, along with land, was granted to noblemen by the king in return for military service in wartime and advice during peace

**totalitarian state** a country run by a dictator who allows no opposition

**tragic flaw** *(hamartia)* a character fault that leads to the protagonist's downfall

**tragic recognition** *(anagnorisis)* recognition of the error of one's ways

**transpose** to move the setting and/or period of a play from its original setting or context to a suitable or parallel context

**trochee** poetic metre in which the stress falls on the first syllable (and then on every other syllable), e.g. 'dum, di' as in 'Thrice the brindled cat hath mewed' *(Act 4, Scene 1)*

**usurper** someone who seizes the crown without the right to do so

**verse** a group or series of groups of written lines, containing a rhythm or rhyme

Great Clarendon Street, Oxford, OX2 6DP,

United Kingdom

Oxford University Press is a department of the University of Oxford.

It furthers the University's objective of excellence in research, scholarship, and education by publishing worldwide. Oxford is a registered trade mark of Oxford University Press in the UK and in certain other countries

British Library Cataloguing in Publication Data

Data available

ISBN 978-0-19-830482-1

10 9 8 7 6 5 4 3

Printed in China by Printplus Ltd.

**Acknowledgements**

**Cover:** Maggie Brodie/Trevillion Images

Photos: **p.6:** dominic dibbs/Alamy; **p.10:** Photostage; **p.12:** PERSSON Johan/ArenaPAL; **p.17:** Photostage; **p.21:** Photostage; **p.24:** Lebrecht Music and Arts Photo Library/Alamy; **p.26:** Geraint Lewis/Alamy; **p.30:** Georgios Kollidas/Shutterstock; **p.33:** Private Collection/ The Bridgeman Art Library; **p.34:** Lance Bellers/Shutterstock; **p.36:** ZUMA Press, Inc./Alamy; **p.39:** Mary Evans Picture Library; **p.42:** Jane Hobson/Alamy; **p.50:** AF archive/Alamy; **p.55:** Photostage; **p.56:** Geraint Lewis/Alamy; **p.60:** Geraint Lewis/Alamy; **p.62:** Nigel Norrington/ArenaPAL; **p.66:** Mary Evans Picture Library/Alamy; **p.70:** Photostage; **p.72:** AF archive/Alamy; **p.73:** drew farrell/Alamy; **p.77:** AF archive/Alamy.

We have tried to trace and contact all copyright holders before publication. If notified, the publishers will be pleased to rectify any errors or omissions at the earliest opportunity.